IMAGES
*of America*

# MEDICINE PARK
## OKLAHOMA'S FIRST RESORT

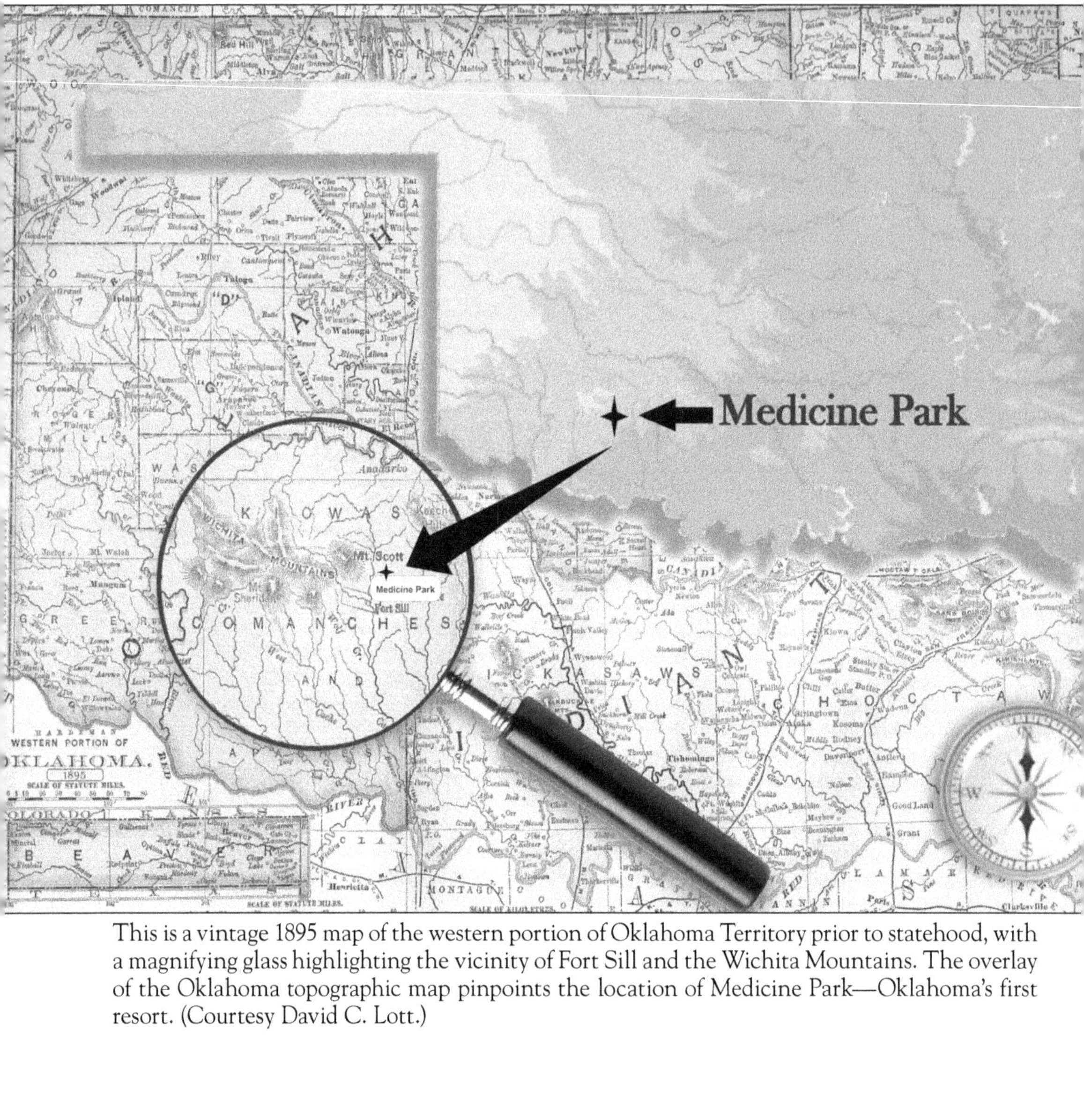


This is a vintage 1895 map of the western portion of Oklahoma Territory prior to statehood, with a magnifying glass highlighting the vicinity of Fort Sill and the Wichita Mountains. The overlay of the Oklahoma topographic map pinpoints the location of Medicine Park—Oklahoma's first resort. (Courtesy David C. Lott.)

ON THE COVER: A model "cowgirl" poses in this professionally staged advertising photograph at the cobblestone entry gate to Merry Circle Cabins. The hillsides of Medicine Park were dotted with a grouping of 27 rental cabins, which were purchased in the early 1940s by Claude Thomas (no relation to town founder Elmer Thomas). The cabins all had individual names, such as Blue Heaven, Redbird, Greenleaf, Winnie Mae, Lady Alice, Auto Inn, and Moon Glow. Claude Thomas also operated Merry Circle Store for many years. Daughter Patrica and her husband, Kenneth King, later operated the business until the late 1980s. (Courtesy of the Jimmy Hysaw Collection, Museum of the Great Plains, Lawton.)

IMAGES
*of America*

# Medicine Park
## Oklahoma's First Resort

David C. Lott

ARCADIA
PUBLISHING

ISBN 978-0-7385-7745-6

Published by Arcadia Publishing
Charleston, South Carolina

Library of Congress Control Number: 2009937002

For all general information contact Arcadia Publishing at:
Telephone 843-853-2070
Fax 843-853-0044
E-mail sales@arcadiapublishing.com
For customer service and orders:
Toll-Free 1-888-313-2665

Visit us on the Internet at www.arcadiapublishing.com

*This book is dedicated to my deceased mother, who always encouraged paths less traveled, and to countless people who have climbed out onto limbs for Medicine Park, then sawed them off to see where the adventures would lead.*

# Contents

# Acknowledgments

There is not any way in the space allotted to tell the entire history of such a colorful little community as Medicine Park. The goal of this book is to provide present and future generations with a brief snapshot of our historic resort community's early development and formative years, and to preserve small glimpses of historical information, timelines, and imagery that may otherwise be lost or forgotten. It is my personal hope, as an advocate for more than two decades for preservation, restoration, and revitalization, that it will serve as a partial reminder of our past challenges and successes as the town journeys through the new century.

I am deeply grateful to numerous individuals, friends, organizations, agencies, and institutions for their assistance.

Thank you to the Museum of the Great Plains in Lawton and John Hernandez, museum director, for providing me with access to the museum's photographic collections. I'm especially grateful to Deborah Baroff, the museum's head curator, for her patience and for assisting me in assembling a large number of the images used. This effort would not have been possible without her.

I wish to thank William "Bill" Whitworth of New Boston, Michigan, for the loan of his extensive vintage Medicine Park postcard collection, which he began collecting some 30 years ago. His collection helped expedite my task in gathering historic images.

I'd like to acknowledge the Medicine Park Telephone Company, Wichita Mountains Wildlife Refuge, and the Oklahoma Department of Wildlife Conservation for allowing me to use selected images from their collections.

I'd also like to thank numerous people who provided me with inspiration, encouragement, information about Medicine Park, and/or photographs from their collections: my longtime Medicine Park friends Louretta Borsos, Bill and Janette Patty, David and Candace McCoy, and lifelong residents Kenneth and Dora Hilliary, Judy Robertson, Melinda Freeman Whitewolf, the Leath family, and Jean Haile. Thanks also go to Paul Fisher of the Park Area Foundation, Glo King Wiley, Marilyn Callaway-Cosgrove, friends Chris Caldwell and Kenneth Gunkel of Lawton, and Glenda Turner, Phyllis Young of Lawton, and Rosetta Wills, daughter of Bob Wills.

I am also grateful to my friends Hank and Lee Sabine for use of their photographs, their friendship, encouragement, and editing; acquisitions editor Ted Gerstle and publisher John Pearson at Arcadia Publishing, for their patience and tolerating my delays.

I'm deeply grateful to all.

# INTRODUCTION

Medicine Park, Oklahoma's first resort, noted for its granite cobblestone architecture, was founded July 4, 1908, by Elmer Thomas, a young lawyer recently elected to the first senate of the new state of Oklahoma. Nearby Fort Sill was established in 1869, and the new city of Lawton and the Wichita Mountains Forest and Game Preserve (now the Wichita Mountains Wildlife Refuge) were established in 1901. Oklahoma achieved statehood on November 16, 1907, becoming the 46th state. Eight months later, Medicine Park Health and Pleasure Resort was founded.

At the dawn of the 20th century, new national forests and national parks were being established across the nation. The idea was an American invention in an effort to preserve scenic lands and conserve wilderness areas. The public held a fascination with America's natural wonders, and a new form of tourism was born. Numerous resorts opened near these park entrances to provide tourists with food, lodging, and entertainment. All of these factors provided the ideal catalyst for Medicine Park's creation. Their histories are, in part, Medicine Park's story.

On September 8, 1901, Elmer Thomas and several companions camped along Medicine Creek near the present-day fish hatchery and came across a deep, granite rock gorge on the creek. Thomas envisioned that it might serve as a site to construct a dam for a water source for the new city of Lawton. He also envisioned the area as a site for a resort, especially since the creek was believed by Native Americans to have healing powers. Through the land office in Lawton, he homesteaded the parcel of land where they had camped. He also found that 880 acres bordering neighboring Fort Sill and the national forest had been filed upon for homesteading but were unclaimed. His law practice was new and he had no money. He sought out Hal Lloyd, a successful businessman from Altus, and they began buying property. But titles were muddled, and it took until 1908 to acquire clear titles.

They hired engineer Capt. Warren Dunbar to survey the property and draw up a plat. The plans included a business district, lots for vacation homes, camping and picnicking areas, and three parks (Assembly Park, Dunbar Peak Park, and Mount Olive Park). The pair formed The Lawton Rapid Transit Railroad Company to own, manage, and promote the venture.

In May 1908, articles began appearing in Lawton newspapers about the new resort. Touted as the "natural health and pleasure grounds of the southwest," the company stated the area would develop into the "most attractive resort east of the Rocky Mountains." The company's proposed rail system would carry passengers the 15 or so miles from Lawton to Medicine Park in just 40 minutes. At the time there was not a highway such as there is today, and the only means to Medicine Park was a wagon road along Medicine Creek through Fort Sill.

When Medicine Park opened on July 4, 1908, it was a gala event with band music, fireworks, picnics, and a limited number of campsites. The initial attraction was a swimming hole called Bath Lake, created by a rock dam on Medicine Creek. A small wooden building, moved from Thomas's homesteaded site, was used as a kitchen. Meals were served under a large surplus army tent.

Lots sized 50-feet-by-140-feet were sold as sites for "cottages where year round outdoor life is at its best." Some lots sold for as little as $16, but the average sale was $60. All money was invested back into the resort for roads, bridges, and improvements. The following year, four small homes were built by members of the Sabine family. Numerous improvements were added, including a bridge spanning the creek, a wooden bathhouse for a changing room, roadways, and Gondola Dam, which created a fishing lake and impounded more water for Bath Lake. Other additions included a large, roofed, open-air pavilion called the Outside Inn, with oak tree trunk support columns and a spacious porch. It even had its own dairy and irrigated vegetable gardens. In 1910, the Medicine Park Clubhouse was built atop Mount Dunbar. It also featured oak tree trunk support columns, a spacious porch and provided the fledgling resort's first sleeping rooms.

The Lawton Rapid Transit Railroad Company never materialized as envisioned. Instead it provided open air "buses." They transported visitors back and forth from Lawton and Fort Sill to Medicine Park for $1 per person each way and 50¢ for trunks.

The new national trend of health resorts performed important social functions. Families flocked to them for vacations and reunions, and individuals patronized them for personal rejuvenation. The resorts were places to see and be seen, enjoy outdoor recreation, rub shoulders with celebrities, be entertained, and make business and political contacts. The development of Medicine Park followed common patterns whereby entrepreneurs developed resorts with hotels and bathhouses to attract visitors, leading to more businesses and population growth. They often established sanitariums containing the latest medical devices, as well as mineral waters, Turkish baths, swimming pools, and other recreational resources.

By 1911, the Oklahoma Press Association, of which Thomas was a member, had a statewide membership of 500. In 1913, the association formed a corporation, sold $10,000 in shares and built their Press Association Clubhouse in Medicine Park. Thomas donated land in exchange for continued publicity. The two-story building opened April 24, 1916. It consisted of a concrete foundation and cobblestones set into concrete support columns, finished by wood framing and a screened-in second floor with flat rooftop garden. The ground floor was used as a social area, and the second floor was equipped with cots and bedding. Lodging was available for members only. Men slept on one side of the large open room, women on the other.

The Medicine Park Fish Hatchery, on land once homesteaded by Thomas, was donated to the state in 1912. It was built using prison labor and opened for operation in 1915. It was the first to service the new Oklahoma Fish and Game Department's needs for stocking of lakes and ponds in the state.

In 1914, Medicine Park was sold to D. L. Sleeper and Associates of Oklahoma City for $16,000. His group enclosed the Outside Inn and added a flat-roofed, wood-framed, two-story hotel. Cobblestone support columns replaced the tree trunk columns. However, they defaulted on their financing in 1915, and Thomas and Lloyd once again had possession of Medicine Park.

Thomas built a two-story annex in 1916 adjacent to the hotel. The first floor, constructed with a facade of cobblestones, was called The Park Store and was operated by Thomas's wife, Edith. The wood-framed second floor served as additional hotel rooms, connected to the main hotel by a breezeway. Improvements were made to Bath Lake, and concession buildings and slides were added.

A small cobblestone building was constructed next to the Park Store, and the first school in Medicine Park was established. The first teacher was Leona Hilliary. As the community grew, more residents became permanent. By 1921, a larger school was needed. Thomas donated materials, labor, and land for a one-room schoolhouse. The new school was located about a block northwest of the hotel. The small cobblestone building, once used as the school, was converted into the Medicine Park Post Office. It remained the post office until 1963, when a new post office building was built in its present location.

Thomas became the sole proprietor of Medicine Park when he bought Lloyd's interest in 1920. He changed the name of his company to the Medicine Park Company, and again made numerous improvements to Medicine Park. He built a spacious dance hall creek-side. Much of Medicine Park was landscaped with beautiful gardens, fountains, trees, footbridges, and grassy areas. In 1920, Thomas selected a prime location, adjacent to the Park Store, to build his permanent home, which exists today. Built almost entirely of cobblestones, the two-story structure featured a sun deck and shallow retention pond on the roof to help cool the cabin in the summer. In the mid-1920s, Parmenter's Apartments were built on West Lake Drive, near Bath Lake, offering an alternative to cabin or lodge rentals.

Elmer Thomas hired Capt. Frank King in the fall of 1921 to resurvey the park and prepare for a public auction to sell remaining lots. A year later, 104 lots were sold at auction.

During this period, there was a growing national trend for health spa treatments, which were commonly prescribed for sufferers of chronic ailments, particularly digestive, arthritic, and skin problems. Therapies using mineralized spring or well water gained huge popularity in the United States.

In 1922, Dr. C. W. Baird, a general practitioner and award-winning tennis player, built Baird's Sanatorium and Health Clinic. It was located creek-side, across from the hotel near the present-day town hall. The wooden two-story building featured his residence, Turkish baths, and a health clinic. There were also clay tennis courts across the street, just east of the hotel. Baird was instrumental in getting state tennis tournaments held in Medicine Park. The spa was liberally patronized by visiting political associates of Senator Thomas. Many lively political discussions were held, and the upper floor was nicknamed the "Little White House." During this era, outlaws mixed with politicians, businessmen, soldiers and officers from Fort Sill, families, and socialites. Many of its patrons tended to be well-to-do, and Medicine Park became known as the "Jewel of the Southwest."

In the late spring of 1926, Medicine Creek flooded. Many structures were damaged, including the bathhouse, swinging bridge, auto bridge, and the creek-side dance hall, but all were soon rebuilt. The rebuilt dance hall's operation was diversified, and it began its use as a skating rink.

On Easter 1926, Lawton's Congregational church members, under the direction of Rev. Anthony Mark Wallock, staged a passion play on a hilltop on the eastern edge of Medicine Park. That first play drew 200 visitors and grew to 500 the next year. In 1930, approximately 6,000 people witnessed Medicine Park's Easter pageant.

In the fall of 1926, Thomas sold Medicine Park to a corporation of doctors. They changed the hotel's name to the Grand Hotel. During this period, the park underwent a transformation away from its original family recreation and pleasure resort. Their period of ownership is filled with legends of widespread gambling, slot machines, bootlegged whiskey, and "pretty girls." This transition did not please Senator Thomas, as it was a far cry from his intent for the park as a place for families.

By July 1930, the Press Association was having difficulty funding its clubhouse and association directors believed it had served its usefulness to the association. It was sold for $4,000 to the Hutchins family of Lawton. The family leased it to Frank Wright, who converted it into the Apache Inn, complete with an elaborate dining area and sleeping rooms. It remained as such until it burned in the 1940s.

In the mid-1930s, a small hydroelectric power plant was built on Gondola Dam by Wolverton Electric. It provided power for the fish hatchery, the hotel, and several local businesses.

Due to the growing popularity of the Easter pageant, in 1934–1935 the Works Progress Administration (WPA) built the present-day Holy City of the Wichitas in the wildlife refuge, 5 miles west of its original location. A $94,000 federal grant authorized by President Roosevelt supported construction. A 1935 ceremony commemorated completion of the outdoor amphitheater and numerous granite structures intended to recreate the Holy Land and serve as a setting for the annual passion play. A transmission line was built from the hydroelectric plant on Gondola Dam to the Holy City to provide electricity for floodlights used during the play.

The doctors' corporation operated Medicine Park until 1939, when Lulabelle Young bought the venture, comprising some 360 acres. She stated, "I wanted to be the only woman to own a town. I bought it for the glory of it." She later became Lulabelle Hutchins after marrying Bob Hutchins. The hotel, which she renamed Medicine Park Lodge, was in a dilapidated state, having been used as a tax shelter for the doctors. She refurbished it and 30 cabins. Through her guidance, the local economy thrived even through World War II. She put people to work during tough times and paid them $1 a day plus meals.

She made improvements to the cabins, renting them by the day, week, or month, built a new swinging bridge, a 110-foot slide, and expanded the bathhouse to include an arcade. She also added a small zoo with monkeys and bears, and made improvements to the dance hall and skating rink. She redecorated the hotel, its Tap Room, dining room, and the Silver Lounge, and had murals painted by Don Blanding, an Oklahoma artist. She also added a 60-foot long stone bar.

Medicine Park's drawing card became weekend dances. Famous bands of the era, such as Pinky Tomblin and Les Brown, delighted audiences. Bob Wills and The Texas Playboys, the kings of western swing, became regulars from 1933 through the 1940s. Numerous other big bands made their way through Medicine Park en route to venues in Oklahoma City, Dallas, and Fort Worth. The Medicine Park Clubhouse on Mount Dunbar was dubbed "The Playboy Club" after the Texas Playboys, who stayed there many times. The Clubhouse fell victim to a fire in the early 1940s.

Following the end of World War II, Lulabelle sold her property three times—always having to take possession again after the new owners defaulted. During this period, one of the owners changed the name of the hotel back to the Grand Hotel and the third story of the hotel and the second story of the annex burned. She sold the property for a final time in 1954 to the Texas Land Company from McAllen, Texas. The transaction was done in part by her trading for land in Texas. They operated as a resort for about three years. However, the urbanization of America was underway and was changing public trends. The company rented parts of the hotel and other properties, including the skating rink, to various business people after 1955. The glory days of Medicine Park as a resort seemed to be fading as the growing pains of becoming a town were becoming more apparent.

During this time, Medicine Park had numerous small businesses, including the Dam Café, Merry Circle with its rental cabins and store, Callaway's Grocery and Market, Medicine Park Service Station, Cecil's Beauty Shop, Park Café, Carpenter's Grocery (later called Haile's Grocery), a laundromat, and Beasley's Service Station.

Beginning in the early 1960s, the town started to experience a variety of social and economic struggles. In 1966, the hotel, which had been closed for a number of years, was leased to Rex and Ruby "Grandma" Leath as an antique shop. Before moving in, they had to haul away 50 bales of hay, 3 loads of sand, and 30 loads of trash—a sharp contrast from the salad days of "Jewel of the Southwest."

Town residents knew that if they were going to keep their community intact, they needed to band together. In 1968, the Comanche County Commissioners were petitioned by residents for an election to vote on incorporating Medicine Park as an Oklahoma town. This action was needed to create a governmental structure that would be able to qualify for federal grants, loans, and generate revenue for loan repayment. The top priority was construction of a municipal sewage collection and treatment system that would eliminate the flow of raw sewage into Medicine Creek. After a successful election effort, the new town was incorporated as the town of Medicine Park on July 30, 1969.

In 1973, the hotel was sold to Rex and "Grandma" Leath. They renamed it the Old Plantation Restaurant. It was listed as The Medicine Park Hotel on the National Register of Historic Places in 1979. The diner, which became the main focus of their business, became known for their burgers, catfish, huge steaks that "hung off the platter," famous rolls, and cold beer. Rex could always be found behind the bar or in the kitchen, Grandma at someone's table telling tall tales, promoting Medicine Park, or giving out her recipe for hot rolls.

Revitalization and restoration efforts for the town began slowly in the early 1990s. Medicine Park celebrated its Centennial on July 4, 2008, and its current population is approximately 400 people. The Wichita Mountains Wildlife Refuge nowadays host more than 1.5 million annual visitors, and is the second most visited national wildlife refuge in America.

# *One*

# Historic Fort Sill

Fort Sill was established in 1869 by Maj. Gen. Philip Sheridan, who led a campaign to stop hostile tribes from raiding settlements in Texas and Kansas. Sheridan's campaign involved six cavalry regiments accompanied by frontier scouts "Buffalo Bill" Cody and "Wild Bill" Hickok. Troops included the famed 7th Cavalry, 19th Kansas Volunteers, and the 10th Cavalry Buffalo Soldiers (a distinguished group of black soldiers) who constructed many of the stone buildings still surrounding the old post quadrangle. It was first called Camp Wichita, but Sheridan later renamed it in honor of Brig. Gen. Joshua Sill, a friend killed during the Civil War. The first Indian agent was Col. Albert Gallatin Boone, grandson of Daniel Boone.

After Fort Sill's establishment, President Grant approved a peace policy placing responsibility for the tribes under Quaker Indian agents. Soldiers were restricted from taking punitive action against the American Indians, who interpreted this as a sign of weakness. They resumed raiding the frontier and used the fort as a sanctuary. Fort Sill's mission became one of law enforcement protecting the American Indians from outlaws, squatters, and cattle rustlers.

In 1874, the Comanches, Kiowas, and Southern Cheyennes went on the warpath. The resulting yearlong Red River War involved relentless pursuit. Without a chance to graze livestock and faced with disappearance of the buffalo, the tribes eventually surrendered. Quanah Parker's Quohada Comanches were the last to abandon the struggle. Their arrival at Fort Sill in June 1875 marked the end of American Indian warfare on the South Plains. In 1894, Apache warrior Geronimo and 341 Apache prisoners of war were brought to Fort Sill. Geronimo was granted permission to travel for a while with Pawnee Bill's Wild West Show. In July 1901, Geronimo was baptized in Medicine Creek by the Methodist Church. He died of pneumonia at Fort Sill in 1909, and the Apaches remained prisoners of war until 1913.

Fort Sill gradually changed from cavalry to field artillery. The first artillery battery arrived in 1902, and the last cavalry regiment departed in 1907. The School of Field Artillery was founded at Fort Sill in 1911 and continues to operate today.

The above image shows officers' quarters under construction at Fort Sill in 1870. Originally called Camp Wichita, there was considerable discussion over the selection of a formal name for the new post. The 7th Calvary wanted it named Fort Elliot, and the 19th Kansas Volunteers called it Camp Starvation. The original occupants, the Comanche and the Kiowa, called it names that meant, "where the soldiers live at Medicine Bluffs." General Sheridan decided on Fort Sill in honor of Brig. Gen. Joshua W. Sill, a West Point classmate who was killed leading the charge at the Battle of Stones River in Tennessee on August 01, 1862. Orders confirming the name Fort Sill were issued July 2, 1869. Below is the Post Trader's Store in 1870. (Both courtesy of Museum of the Great Plains.)

The above image shows the north line of Fort Sill's officers' quarters, 1872. The first post commander was Bvt. Maj. Gen. Benjamin Grierson. In 1871, during the peace policy period issued by President Grant, soldiers were restricted from taking punitive action against the American Indians, who took this as a sign of weakness and resumed raiding the Texas frontier and used Fort Sill as a sanctuary. In 1871 General of the Army William Tecumseh Sherman arrived at Fort Sill to find several Kiowa chiefs boasting about a wagon train massacre. When Sherman ordered their arrest during a meeting on Grierson's porch, two of them attempted to assassinate him. In memory of the event, the commanding general's quarters were dubbed Sherman House. It is the middle house in the photograph. Below is the Sherman House as it is today. (Both courtesy of Museum of the Great Plains.)

Pictured here in 1888 are members of Troop C of the 5th Cavalry at Fort Sill. One of their predominant missions was to patrol the western portion of Oklahoma Territory and arrest boomers and squatters prior to the opening of Oklahoma lands to settlement. (Courtesy of Museum of the Great Plains.)

Troops E, F, H, and K of the 7th Calvary and troops D and L of the 5th Calvary are shown on the Parade Grounds of Fort Sill, 1890. (Courtesy of Museum of the Great Plains.)

Fort Sill is seen here in the late 1880s. The buffalo soldiers of the 9th and 10th Cavalries were stationed at Fort Sill in the late 1870s and provided major assistance in the construction of the post. (Courtesy of Museum of the Great Plains.)

Shown here is the Red Store, just south of Fort Sill, 1904. In a conference that lasted four days in October 1892, a delegation of government officials called the Cherokee Commission, persuaded Comanche and Kiowa leaders to sell their land to the government so that it might be homesteaded. Ultimately they relinquished their lands for $1.25 an acre. Each American Indian, in addition to his share of the proceeds, was to receive an allotment of 160 acres, the money and lands held in a trust for a period of 20 years. The agreement became known as the Jerome Agreement. (Courtesy of Museum of the Great Plains.)

Quanah Parker was the last chief of the Comanches. Suspicious of whites from previous experiences with lies and deceptive treaties, Quanah decided to remain on the warpath, raiding in Texas and Mexico and outmaneuvering the army. He was almost killed during an attack at Adobe Walls in the Texas Panhandle in 1874. The U.S. Army was relentless in its Red River War of 1874–1875. Quanah's tribe was weary and starving. On June 2, 1875, he and his band surrendered at Fort Sill. He quickly acclimated himself to the white culture by learning Spanish and English, adopting new agricultural methods, and promoting American Indian education. He prospered as both a farmer and the managing agent for business deals between whites and American Indian tribes. He was reputed in later years to be the wealthiest American Indian in North America. In 1886 he became a judge of the Court of Indian Affairs. In 1890, he was principal chief of all Comanche bands. He rode beside Geronimo in the inaugural parade of Pres. Theodore Roosevelt in 1905. Quanah Parker died on February 23, 1911, and is buried at Chief's Knoll on Fort Sill. (Courtesy of Museum of the Great Plains.)

Geronimo was an Apache warrior. In 1876, the army tried to move the Chiricahua Apaches onto a reservation in Arizona, but Geronimo fled to Mexico, eluding troops for a decade. The last few months of the campaign required 5,000 soldiers and 500 scouts to track down Geronimo and his band of 16 warriors, 12 women, and 6 children. Exhausted and outnumbered, Geronimo surrendered in 1886. Geronimo and 450 Apaches were shipped by boxcar to Florida for imprisonment, and they were relocated to Fort Sill in 1894. On July 1, 1903, Geronimo was baptized into the Methodist Church in Medicine Creek. The event was witnessed by Quanah Parker and Medicine Park's founder Elmer Thomas. In his later years, he became a celebrity and toured with Wild West shows and other expositions. He rode with Quanah Parker in Pres. Theodore Roosevelt's inaugural parade in 1905. Geronimo died of pneumonia on February 17, 1909, and is buried in the Apache cemetery at Fort Sill. (Courtesy of Museum of the Great Plains.)

The School of the Field Artillery was founded in 1911 and continues to operate today as the U.S. Army Field Artillery Center. In this photograph, Fort Sill troops train on a .75 mm field gun during World War I. Fort Sill has served variously as home to the Infantry school of Musketry, the School for Aerial Observers, the Air Service Flying School, and Army Aviation School. Fort Sill is the only active army installation of all the forts built on the South Plains during the Indian Wars. (Courtesy of Museum of the Great Plains.)

Pictured here is the balloon hangar at Fort Sill in 1918. Balloons, which could carry personnel aloft to heights of thousands of feet, had an impact on artillery philosophy at Fort Sill as they silently observed and directed artillery fire. The first military aviation unit arrived for duty in 1915. Construction of an airfield was begun in August 1917 and was completed in September 1917. It was named in honor of Lt. Henry Post, who had been killed in 1914 while attempting to establish a record altitude of 12,120 feet. (Courtesy of Museum of the Great Plains.)

# *Two*

# Wichita Mountains National Forest and Game Preserve

The Wichita Mountains are among the oldest mountain ranges on earth. Formation began 600 million years ago, when eroded silts followed by volcanic uplift were deposited into a sea. As mountains considerably higher than today's formed, the sea eventually subsided. Erosion over hundreds of millions of years stripped off mountaintops, until all that remains today are weather-reduced domes.

The word Wichita derives from two ancient American Indian words: *weets*, meaning "man," and *ee-taw* meaning "of the north." In the 1600s, Spanish traders bartered with Wichita Indians for hides. French traders during the 1770s were the first to name the mountains. Col. Henry Dodge was the first American to make contact with native tribes in 1834, when he and his troops entered the area to halt American Indian raids on the Santa Fe Trail.

In booming Oklahoma Territory in August 1901, President McKinley claimed a portion of the Wichita Mountains, from the Comanche-Kiowa-Apache Indian Reservation, as the Wichita Forest Reserve. By this time, overhunting and disease had reduced the American bison in all of America from 60 million to only two small wild herds, numbering about 550 animals. Farsighted conservationists became concerned for their pending extinction. In 1905, Pres. Theodore Roosevelt, a conservationist, issued a proclamation renaming this area the Wichita National Forest and Game Preserve and creating the nation's first big-game animal and wildlife preserve.

In 1905, the American Bison Society demanded buffalo be given protection. Through their efforts, the New York Zoological Society offered 15 bison to the new Wichita National Forest and Game Preserve. Congress set aside $15,000, and 15 bison were shipped by rail from New York to Cache, Oklahoma, on October 11, 1907. Seven days later, these six bulls and nine cows were returned to the plains. People flocked into the Wichitas to welcome their return, including many mounted braves who came to see the bison that had provided meat and shelter for countless generations.

The area was later transferred in 1935 to the Bureau of Biological Survey, a predecessor agency of the present-day Fish and Wildlife Service, for administration under the national wildlife refuge program. It is now known today as the Wichita Mountains Wildlife Refuge and encompasses 59,020 acres.

Here is the entrance gate to the Wichita National Forest and Game Preserve in 1905. (Courtesy of Museum of the Great Plains.)

The New York Zoological Society corrals 15 of the finest bison at the Bronx Zoo in New York City by in preparation for a more 1,500-mile journey to Oklahoma. (Courtesy of U.S. Fish and Wildlife Service-Wichita Mountains Wildlife Refuge.)

On October 11, 1907, the bison were individually crated and loaded onto a train bound for Cache, Oklahoma. William Hornaday, the first director of the Wildlife Conservation Society (then the New York Zoological Society), and members of the American Bison Society sponsored and supervised the operation. (Courtesy of Museum of the Great Plains.)

On October 18, 1907, the bison arrived from New York at the railhead in Cache, Oklahoma. There was great excitement in the little town when the train pulled in with the heavily crated buffalo. The great Comanche chief Quanah Parker was among those who came to the station. (Courtesy of U.S. Fish and Wildlife Service-Wichita Mountains Wildlife Refuge.)

October 18, 1907, the 15 individual crates containing the bison were transferred to wagons to be hauled the 13 miles to their new home in Wichita National Forest and Game Preserve. (Courtesy of U.S. Fish and Wildlife Service-Wichita Mountains Wildlife Refuge.)

October 18, 1907, hundreds of people gathered in the Wichita National Forest and Game Preserve to see the bison and watch as they were turned free from their travel crates. (Courtesy of Museum of the Great Plains.)

Among the crowd in the game preserve on October 18, 1907, were dozens of mounted American Indian braves who came to see the great bison—which had provided food, shelter and clothing to their ancestors for many centuries—returned to their homeland. (Courtesy of U.S. Fish and Wildlife Service-Wichita Mountains Wildlife Refuge.)

October 18, 1907, the 15 bison are finally free once again to roam their native prairies. This was the first animal reintroduction in North American history. (Courtesy of Bill Whitworth.)

Originally indigenous to the Wichita Mountains, elk were extinct in the area by the late 1800s. In 1911, five Rocky Mountain elk, comprised of one bull and four cows, were transplanted from the National Elk Refuge herd in Jackson, Wyoming. In 1912, an additional 15 Rocky Mountain elk (3 bulls and 12 cows) were received from the same herd and brought by trucks into the game preserve. The elk now inhabiting the refuge are descended from these animals. (Courtesy of Museum of the Great Plains.)

One of the game preserve's early fire crews is pictured with its water wagon around 1910. Pictured from left to right are Bert Cook, Frank Rush, Herbert Hodge, and Homer Edwards. (Courtesy of Museum of the Great Plains.)

The game preserve fire crew in March 1908 included, from left to right, Herbert Hodge, Bert Cook, Frank Rush, and Homer Edwards. Professionals regularly use prescribed fire as a management tool. They are carefully controlled and applied only under predetermined conditions to ensure the desired results are achieved. (Courtesy of Museum of the Great Plains.)

Dr. J. Allen Perisho is shown standing beside his 1915 Studebaker at the entrance to the Wichita National Forest and Game Preserve. On the board to the right of the gate, several reward signs are posted as warnings to poachers. (Courtesy of Museum of the Great Plains.)

An unidentified tourist poses in 1920 beside her automobile under the cobblestone gateway entrance into the Wichita National Forest and Game Preserve. (Courtesy of Museum of the Great Plains.)

In 1933, the Civilian Conservation Corps (CCC) was begun in an effort to provide work for young men during the Great Depression, and at the same time accomplish much-needed conservation work on public lands. It became the most popular of President Roosevelt's New Deal programs, providing economic relief and training for three million men. The CCC established three camps in the game preserve. They built dams on streams and fencing to improve management of game herds. In this photograph, members of the CCC are building fences. (Courtesy of U.S. Fish and Wildlife Service-Wichita Mountains Wildlife Refuge.)

Eligibility for the CCC was simple: men had to be of sound physical fitness, unemployed, unmarried, and aged 18–26. They were paid $30 a month, with mandatory $25 allotment checks sent to their families, which made life a little easier for people at home. The CCC constructed recreation facilities and numerous buildings and ranger cabins. In this photograph, CCC members are constructing the headquarters building. The CCC program ended in 1942. (Courtesy of U.S. Fish and Wildlife Service-Wichita Mountains Wildlife Refuge.)

At 2,464 feet, Mount Scott, named after Gen. Winfield Scott, is the second tallest mountain in the refuge and the third tallest in the state. Scott was an army general and an unsuccessful presidential candidate in the Whig party in 1852. Known as "Old Fuss and Feathers" and the "Grand Old Man of the Army," he served on active duty as a general longer than any other man in American history. Many historians rate him the ablest American commander of his time. (Courtesy of David C. Lott.)

Mount Scott is a legendary site that boasts tales of ancient spirits, Spanish gold, and buried outlaw loot. Building a two-lane, winding corkscrew road 3 miles up to the summit of Mount Scott necessitated blasting through granite walls 20–60 feet high. The majority of the road had to be cut through the granite using dynamite and nitroglycerin charges. It was hard and dangerous work. The road to Mount Scott's peak officially opened in 1938. It was a joint project of the Public Works Administration, a private firm, and the WPA. Hundreds of thousands of people today drive to the summit, which offers breathtaking views of southwest Oklahoma and Medicine Park. (Both courtesy of U.S. Fish and Wildlife Service-Wichita Mountains Wildlife Refuge.)

# *Three*

# Lawton's Founding

The town site of Lawton was founded August 6, 1901, when the Kiowa-Comanche-Apache reservation, the last of the American Indian lands in the Oklahoma Territory, was opened for settlement by the federal government. In contrast to land runs used in other parts of the Oklahoma Territory, a lottery was established to distribute lands in 160-acre plots in two districts. Both were formed from lands that had once belonged to the three tribes. The northern area, the El Reno District, included the new counties of Kiowa and Hobart. The southern area near Fort Sill, the Lawton District, was then called Lawton County and later renamed Comanche County.

A person wanting a claim had to register for the drawing. On July 10, 1901, registration opened at Fort Sill. During the 16-day registration, about 29,000 prospective homesteaders from all over the United States registered. Another 135,000 registered at El Reno. The drawings for all lands began July 29 at El Reno and lasted four days. On August 6, winners of the Lawton District lottery claimed their 160-acre plots outside the town site in the order that their names were drawn.

The Lawton town site was located on a section of prairie south of Fort Sill. Lots within the original 320-acre area were sold at public auction before a crowd of 40,000 people, with a total of 1,422 lots up for sale. No one was allowed to camp on the town site prior to the auction; they had to wait outside of town. Over 400 businesses set up tents to sell provisions to the settlers. Some men made small buildings on wheels, and after they bought lots in Lawton, they rolled their buildings to their town sites. People registered, putting $25 down to be able to bid for a lot. If their bid won, they had 30 minutes to pay for the lot. If they did not pay, they lost their deposit and the lot was resold. Soon after the auction, an estimated 25,000 townspeople lived in tents for many months, busy building homes and businesses in the new town.

This picture was taken July 10, 1901, at Fort Sill, Oklahoma. Some 29,000 prospective homesteaders from all around the United States showed up and registered during the 16-day registration period at Fort Sill for lands in the Lawton District. The land offices opened at 9:00 a.m. on July 10, 1901, and closed at 6:00 p.m. on July 26. The formal drawing was held in El Reno on July 29, 1901. (Courtesy of Museum of the Great Plains.)

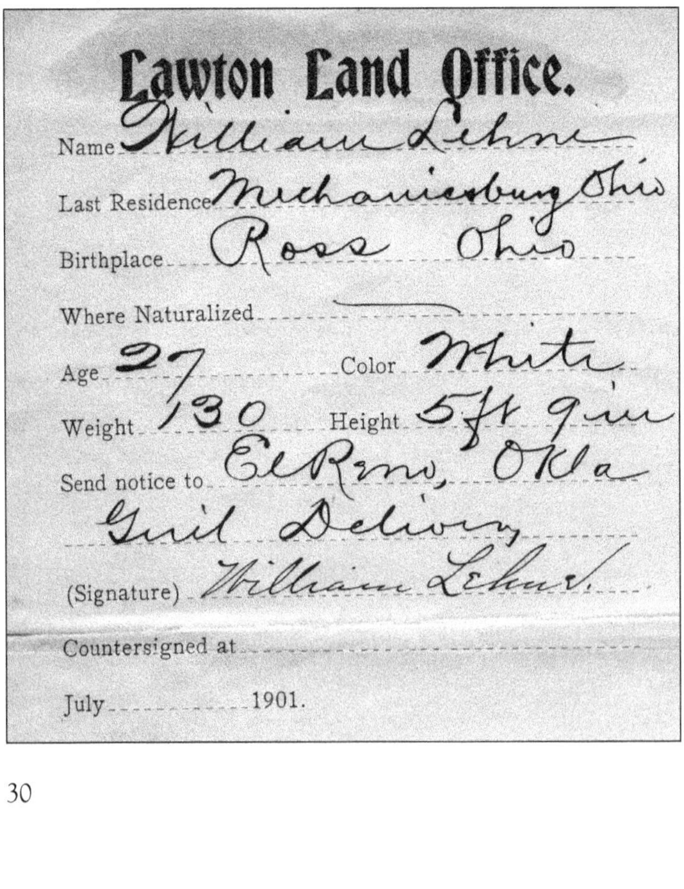

**Lawton Land Office.**

Name William Lehne

Last Residence Mechanicsburg Ohio

Birthplace Ross Ohio

Where Naturalized —

Age 27 Color White

Weight 130 Height 5 ft 9 in

Send notice to El Reno, Okla

Genl Delivery

(Signature) William Lehne

Countersigned at

July 1901.

Pictured here is the 1901 land lottery form of William Lehne, age 27. Potential homesteaders for 160-acre plots had to sign up in person. Single men over the age of 21, men who were the heads of households, and single women could register. Everyone who signed up had to be a U.S. citizen or sign a form saying he or she intended to become a citizen. The forms were guarded and transported to Citizens State Bank of El Reno. (Courtesy of Museum of the Great Plains.)

July 29, 1901, over 100,000 people were at El Reno the first day of the drawing. A platform 32 feet wide was erected in the streets of the city. A box for the El Reno district was placed on one table; a box for the Lawton district was placed on another. Both boxes had iron bars running through them. With the bars, the boxes could be turned around and around to mix up the slips. The officials tried very hard to make sure the drawing was fair, by having 10 blindfolded boys under the age of 18 take turns drawing envelopes from both of the boxes. First they drew from the El Reno box, then from the Lawton box. The commissioner yelled out the name and address on the slip. A total of 500 names were drawn on the first day. Names were drawn every day for the next three days. The final count was 7,737 claims filed at Lawton, and 6,843 claims filed at El Reno. (Courtesy of Museum of the Great Plains.)

This photograph was taken August 1, 1901. Thousands showed up at the Lawton Land Office to file the claim they had won in El Reno. People who had their names drawn were sent postcards that told them when to come to the land office to file their claim. If someone did not show up on the assigned day, the clerks skipped their number. They were given a second chance at the end of the day, and if they still were not present, they lost their claim. Lands not claimed were auctioned off on later dates through October. (Courtesy of Museum of the Great Plains.)

Lawton held its land auction August 1, 1901. The original town site was 320 acres, with a total of 66 blocks. The platted business district had 32 business lots to a block with 27 blocks. Block 39 was set aside for the courthouse. Blocks 18 and 31 were set aside for schools. There were 16 residential lots to a block, with 36 blocks set aside as residential. A total of 1,422 lots went to the highest bidders. (Courtesy of Museum of the Great Plains.)

Here is an early saloon in Lawton, made of tent canvas stretched over a wood frame. Bottled beer sold for 15¢. The "All Nations Welcome but Carrie" sign refers to Carrie Nation, famous for her temperance movement, which opposed alcohol in pre-Prohibition days. Noted for promoting her viewpoint through vandalism, she would march into a bar alone or accompanied by hymn-singing women, singing and praying while smashing fixtures and stock with a hatchet. Between 1900 and 1910, she was arrested 30 times for "hatchetations." (Courtesy of Museum of the Great Plains.)

Like many of Lawton's early businesses, the first post office was established in a tent. Route delivery to homes, businesses, and rural areas from the post office began in April 1904. (Courtesy of Museum of the Great Plains.)

The Keegan Hotel was one of the first facilities for lodging built in downtown Lawton. Records show that prior to 1921, Margaret Keegan was the owner of lots 1, 2, 3, and 4 on block 62 in Lawton. Prior to his death in 1909, famed Apache warrior Geronimo was known to sit on the front porch of the hotel, where he peddled handmade bows and arrows, photographs and his crudely scrawled autographs to make a little money. At times, he would sell out of his artifacts and reportedly tell his "customers" that all he had was a button that had fallen off of his wool navy peacoat, and would then sell them the button for $1. Little did they know he had a whole pocket full of such buttons. (Courtesy of Museum of the Great Plains.)

# *Four*

# The Need for Water

Lawton began addressing crucial issues almost as soon as the city was created, however other priorities took precedence over a permanent source of water. August 1901 was miserably hot. People needed water, and there were no wells within the new city limits. However, there was Cache Creek to the east. Water wagons brought water to thirsty residents, but it wasn't free. Water wagons charged various rates, until the cost stabilized at 25 to 50 ¢ per barrel. The lack of water led to a typhoid outbreak in the city's first year, and there were constant threats of fire. The need for water became critical, and shortages profound. Businesses kept a barrel of water in each establishment in case of fire. City leaders realized that they needed a large, permanent source.

In 1902, Congress awarded Lawton $150,000 for water works, sewers, and schools. In late 1903, two reservoirs were constructed northeast of town, each holding 86,000 gallons to be used in case of fire. Water for domestic use was supplied by new wells, dug northeast of town. Lawton grew and faced more water shortages. In the dry summer of 1906, it was evident the water system was still inadequate. If the needs of thirsty Lawtonians were not enough incentive, the federal government provided more. Enlargement of Fort Sill depended on an adequate water supply.

In September 1901, Elmer Thomas and several companions were camping along Medicine Creek and came across a deep, narrow granite gorge while exploring. Thomas had envisioned it might serve as a site for a dam and water source for Lawton. He also envisioned the creek area as a new resort.

In 1906, Thomas propositioned the City of Lawton, offering to supply 120 acres of his land for a dam site, if the city would, in turn, furnish water for his resort. On the original resort plat, he had even mapped out Lake Medicine (later called Lake La-Ton-Ka and then Lake Lawtonka). Lawton rejected the idea, and seized his land through the right of eminent domain, a process of condemning. Finally a district court jury gave Thomas $3,000, and a later appeal to the state supreme court gave him $1,000 more.

Just prior to the founding of the city of Lawton and the Wichita Mountains National Forest and Game Preserve in 1901, Comanche Indians had a large camp on lands that are now present-day Lake Lawtonka. The Kiowa Indians also had a nearby encampment near Mount Scott. (Courtesy of Museum of the Great Plains.)

By late 1905, the need for water in Lawton had become dire, and resources were inadequate for the growing community and Fort Sill. In early 1906, city officials from Lawton visited the site of present-day Lake Lawtonka Dam on Medicine Creek as proposed by Elmer Thomas. A survey of the site was made by John D. Kennard, city engineer. However, rather than agreeing to Thomas's offer of the land in exchange for water for his coming resort, they condemned the land. (Courtesy of Museum of the Great Plains.)

Construction of Lawton's first dam on Medicine Creek began and was completed in 1906. The 16-foot-tall dam was constructed of large native granite rock boulders and concrete mortar. A 16-inch pipeline was laid from the dam to Lawton. The dam, pipeline, and land right of way cost the city approximately $177,000, of which $60,000 was government funds. With the dam in place, water began to fill Medicine Creek north of the structure creating a lake. However, within just two years, this increased water supply proved to be still inadequate. (Both courtesy of Museum of the Great Plains.)

In 1907, a group takes in the views from the top of the first granite rock and concrete mortar Lake La-ton-ka Dam (later changed to Lake Lawtonka) on Medicine Creek. (Courtesy of Museum of the Great Plains.)

By 1909, the increased water supply provided by the 16-foot-tall dam proved to be inadequate for Lawton. The dam was raised to a height of 50 feet at a cost of $74,780. The City of Lawton then purchased 3,240 acres of land to be included in the lake basin at a cost of $65,000. (Courtesy of Museum of the Great Plains.)

In 1910, late winter and spring rains came, filling the basin and backing water up into Medicine Creek for several miles. The dam overflowed, cascading over the rocks below and there seemed to be an inexhaustible supply. For several years the people of Lawton felt they had a water resource that was great enough to stand any future growth that the city or Fort Sill might require. The winter of 1911 was particularly cold, and water overflowing the 50-foot-tall dam froze. (Both courtesy of Bill Whitworth.)

In 1911, an unknown group poses for a photograph as they are seated and standing on the overflow relief valve at the base of Lake Lawtonka Dam. (Courtesy of Museum of the Great Plains.)

A group of women from the Pioneer Telephone Company poses in 1911 for a photograph on Lake Gondola in Medicine Park, just below the 50-foot-tall Lake Lawtonka Dam. (Courtesy of Phyllis Young.)

The water from Lake La-ton-ka had seemed adequate for Lawton and Fort Sill. Then World War I came, and Camp Doniphan was established. An estimated 50,000 new troops began training at Fort Sill. Bonds in the amount of $375,000 were approved, and in 1918, the height of the dam was raised by 10 feet, and a new, larger 24-foot pipeline built. The entire dam was reinforced from top to bottom to withstand the pressure of the additional water to be impounded. It was now 52 feet wide at the base, 18 feet thick through the central section, 10 feet wide at the top and 375 feet in length. The lake basin now had a capacity of more than 10 billion gallons of water, covering 1408 acres to an average depth of 18 feet—more than doubling its former capacity. With the pipeline's gravity flow, operating costs were low. In 1921, a flat rate of $1 per month was charged for domestic water use and a graduated rate for commercial use. The final step in making the system complete was the installation of a water treatment plant just below the dam in Medicine Park. The original cost of the plant was $140,000. (Courtesy of Bill Whitworth.)

By the early 1920s, the resort of Medicine Park was bustling with activity. Lake La-ton-ka had become an important attraction for visitors as well as a vital water supply for Lawton and Fort Sill. A small wooden passenger boat called *Miss Lawton*, with a brightly colored canvas canopy, offered brief excursion rides on Lake La-ton-ka. The tour offered beautiful views of Mount Scott and the surrounding Wichita Mountains. Most of the boat rides would originate and return to locations at or near the dam. (Both courtesy of Medicine Park Telephone Company.)

# *Five*

# SEN. ELMER THOMAS

Elmer Thomas was born September 8, 1876, and became one of Oklahoma's the most influential political leaders during the state's first four decades. Medicine Park owes its very existence to his vision. After studying law in his birth state of Indiana, Thomas bought a train ticket to Oklahoma City, arriving November 16, 1900. He soon began practicing law in Oklahoma Territory. In late July 1901, Thomas moved to what was to become the town of Lawton and was there for the August 6 opening for settlement. On September 24, 1902, he married Edith Smith, daughter of Judge Wilford M. Smith of South Dakota. They had one child, Wilford Smith Thomas, born in 1904.

Thomas was elected to the first Oklahoma Senate in 1907, where he helped secure funding for the state capitol building. He also helped establish the state game and fish department, donating land for the state's first fish hatchery at Medicine Park. In 1922, he was elected as a Democrat to the U.S. House of Representatives. He was elected to the U.S. Senate in 1926, where he maintained a keen interest in American Indian affairs and farm problems. He sponsored American Indian education measures and the Farm Relief Bill expanding farm credit. Following 1929, as the Great Depression intensified, he advocated paying soldier bonuses, liberalizing Federal Reserve policies, and currency expansion. An enthusiastic New Dealer, he crafted what became known as the Thomas Amendment to the Agricultural Adjustment Act of 1933. He transformed dust into lakes, sponsored public works projects, and secured the location for Tinker Air Force Base. He once said, "I can get money for a dam easier than for my own breakfast."

During World War II, Thomas was entrusted with knowledge of the Manhattan Project, the top-secret development of the atomic bomb. His subcommittee once met in Medicine Park regarding the project that would ultimately bring an end to World War II. By 1948, Thomas ranked third in Senate seniority. He witnessed the Nuremberg War Trials, and in 1949 he toured European capitols, auditing Marshall Plan reconstruction. Thomas left the Senate in 1951, opened a law office in Washington, D.C., and served as a delegate to the 1952 Democratic National Convention. "The Sage of Medicine Park" retired to Lawton in 1957 and died there September 19, 1965.

A 33-year-old Elmer Thomas stands in front of his prized Outside Inn pavilion in the new resort of Medicine Park in 1909. Thomas was an avid fisherman; he is shown here displaying a bass fish he had caught in Medicine Creek. Fishing was an activity he enjoyed throughout his life. (Courtesy of Museum of the Great Plains.)

Elmer Thomas, pictured here in 1920, served in the Oklahoma Senate from 1907–1920, serving as president pro tempore of the Senate from 1910–1913. He was elected to the 68th and 69th U.S. Congresses in 1923 at the age of 47. He was elected to the U.S. Senate in 1926. He knew Quanah Parker and witnessed Geronimo's Christian baptism. A defender of American Indian rights, Thomas secured the title to oil royalties in the bed of the Red River for the Kiowa, Comanche, and Apache tribes, chaired the Committee on Indian Affairs from 1935 to 1944, and co-authored the Oklahoma Indian Welfare Act of 1936. (Courtesy of Museum of the Great Plains.)

Thomas (second from the left) maintained a keen interest in European geopolitics. A supporter of the League of Nations, the World Court, and the Kellogg-Briand Peace Pact in 1927 and 1928, he visited Paris as a delegate to the Inter-Parliamentary Union. He voted for neutrality legislation in 1935 and 1937, but proclaimed American military preparedness his main concern. In June 1938, he became chair of the Committee on Military Appropriations, and after inspecting bases found American defenses "in critical condition." (Courtesy of Museum of the Great Plains.)

If the biggest public man in the inflation fight was Senator Thomas, the biggest private man in the fight was Fr. Charles Edward Coughlin of Detroit. The two are pictured together on cover of the January 15, 1934, issue of *Time* magazine. The Thomas amendment to the Agricultural Adjustment Act of 1933 combined four major inflation suggestions into one omnibus measure and granted the president permissive powers to use none, one, or any combination of inflation techniques to combat the Great Depression. After meeting with Thomas, the president accepted the amendment, and it became part of the "One Hundred Days" legacy of the Roosevelt administration. (Courtesy of David C. Lott.)

By the late 1940s, Thomas ranked third in Senate seniority. He chaired the Committee on Agriculture and Forestry from 1944 to 1946, and again from 1949 to 1950. In 1950, the 74-year-old Elmer Thomas ran for reelection against a much younger A. S. "Mike" Monroney, losing by 14,653 votes. Leaving the Senate, Thomas opened a law office in Washington and served as a delegate to the 1952 Democratic National Convention. Senator Thomas retired to Lawton in 1957 and died there September 19, 1965. (Courtesy of Museum of the Great Plains.)

# *Six*

# Founding of Oklahoma's First Resort

In May 1908, publicity began appearing in Lawton newspapers about the new resort of Medicine Park. Touted as the "natural health and pleasure grounds of the southwest," it stated the area would develop into the "most attractive resort east of the Rocky Mountains." Elmer Thomas and Hal Lloyd's company proposed a rail system that would carry passengers from Lawton to Medicine Park in just 40 minutes. According to James Arthur Manning, "at the time, the only way to reach Medicine Park was a wagon road down Medicine Creek through Shady Lane on down to Four Mile Crossing, then through Fort Sill."

When the resort opened on July 4, 1908, it was a gala event with band music, fireworks, picnics, and a limited number of campsites. The initial attraction was the Bath Lake swimming hole on Medicine Creek, created by a rock dam to impound water. A small wooden building, which had been moved from Thomas's homesteaded site, was used as a kitchen. Meals were served under a large surplus army tent.

Lots measuring 50-feet-by-140-feet were sold as sites for "cottages where year round outdoor life is at its best." Some lots sold for as little as $16, although the average sale price was $60. All money was invested back into the park for roads, bridges, and improvements, such as a creek-side wooden bathhouse, Gondola Dam, which created a fishing lake, and the Outside Inn pavilion.

Through Elmer Thomas' connections, the resort enjoyed a great deal of publicity, and the area began to take on the feel of a resort.

In 1914, Medicine Park was sold to D. L. Sleeper and Associates of Oklahoma City. They defaulted on the loan in 1915, and Thomas and Lloyd once again had possession of Medicine Park. In 1916, they built a two-story annex adjacent to the hotel, and the first floor was called the Park Store. Thomas became the sole proprietor of Medicine Park when he bought out Lloyd's interest in 1920. He changed the name of his company to the Medicine Park Company and made numerous improvements, including the addition of a third story. Thomas selected a prime location adjacent to the Park Store in 1920 to begin construction of his permanent home, which still exists today.

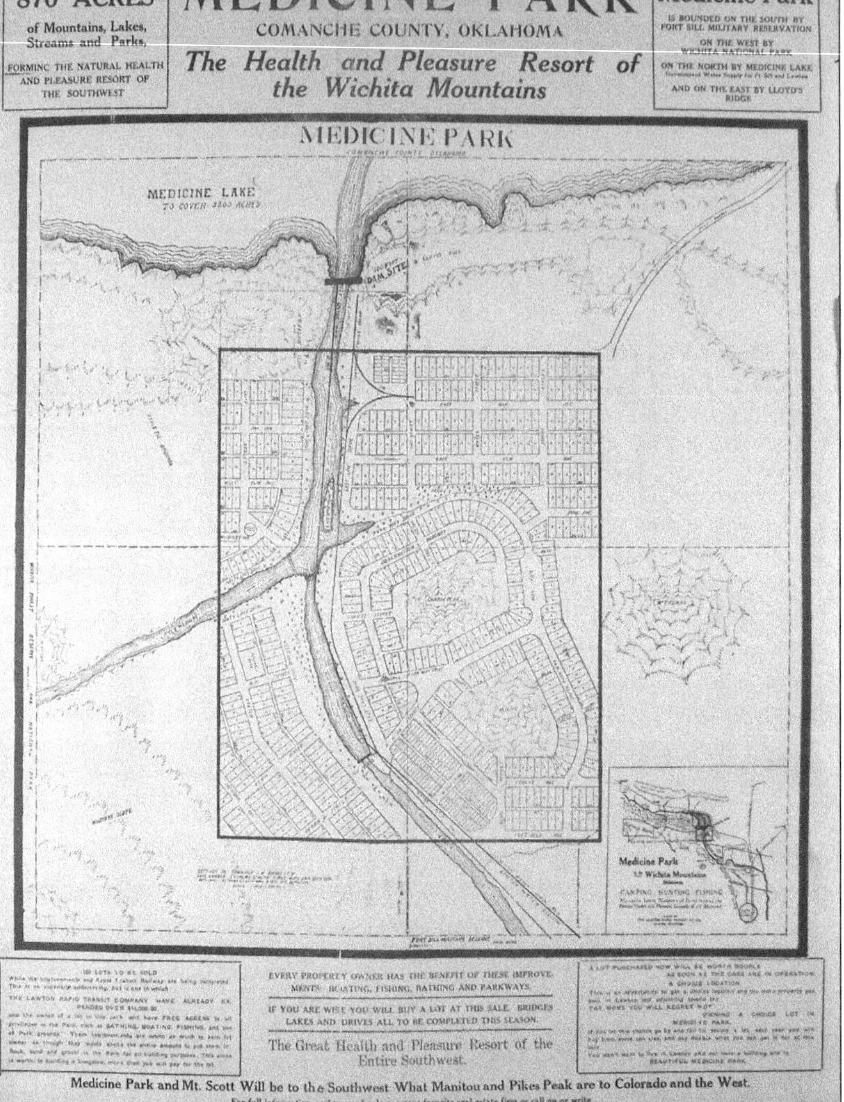


A full-page advertisement in the May 29, 1908, Lawton *Daily News Republican* promotes, "Medicine Park—The Health and Pleasure Resort of the Southwest." The ad touts, "870 acres of mountains, lakes, streams and parks . . . bounded on the south by Fort Sill Military Reservation, on the west by Wichita National Park, on the north by Medicine Lake, government water supply for Fort Sill and Lawton, and on the east by Lloyd's Ridge." The ad further states, "Medicine Park and Mount Scott will be to the southwest what Manitou and Pikes Peak are to Colorado and the West." In the lower left corner, it states, "100 lots will be sold while the improvements and Rapid Transit Railway are being completed. This is no visionary undertaking, but is one that the Lawton Rapid Transit company has already expended over $15,000. The owners of a lot in the park will have free access to all privileges in the park such as bathing, boating, fishing and use of park grounds." It further proclaims, "Lots purchased now will be worth double when the railway cars are in operation." (Courtesy of Museum of the Great Plains.)

Late in the summer of 1908, shortly after the July 4 opening, visitors to the new Medicine Park resort find a fishing hole along Medicine Creek. They appear to be enjoying an afternoon of fishing and having a picnic. (Courtesy of Bill Whitworth.)

Improving roads, streets, and drainage in Medicine Park was an ongoing process. The company poured all money made from lot sales back into improvements. In this photograph is East Lake Drive, as it runs along the creek near the bathhouse and springhouse. A small bridge has been constructed to allow hillside drainage to flow into Medicine Creek. (Courtesy of Museum of the Great Plains.)

Medicine Park was becoming a popular day trip destination for visitors from Lawton and Fort Sill. People wanted to swim in Medicine Creek, enjoy nature, and fish in the creek. They also needed to be fed. Elmer Thomas built the Outside Inn pavilion (on the right), which served as an "indoor" dining area for patrons. (Courtesy of Museum of the Great Plains.)

By 1909, Medicine Park began taking on the feel of a resort. The long structure on the far right is the Outside Inn, where meals were served. The tent next door was the kitchen and small white frame house that served as the land office. It had been Elmer Thomas's house, which he had moved to the site from his homestead. The cobblestone cottage with the porch was one of four built by the Sabine family. The long structure on the left was the bathhouse on Medicine Creek. (Courtesy of Museum of the Great Plains.)

The Bath Lake swimming hole on Medicine Creek was an instant success for Medicine Park. The summers of 1908–1911 were some of the hottest on record, and visitors enjoyed cooling down in the water. The bathhouse provided them with a place to change into their swimming clothes or dress after they had enjoyed their swim. (Courtesy of Bill Whitworth.)

The resort of Medicine Park was growing as cabins and cottages began dotting the hillsides in 1910. Elmer Thomas realized the need for overnight lodging for these visitors, so the Medicine Park Clubhouse was built atop Mount Dunbar (upper left). The Outside Inn (middle right) continued serving meals, and numerous improvements were made to the swimming hole. (Courtesy of Museum of the Great Plains.)

In 1910, the Medicine Park Clubhouse opened on Mount Dunbar, providing a limited amount of lodging for visitors to Medicine Park. It had one large open room with dining tables and chairs in the center, and cots with bedding set up along the walls. A large draw curtain divided the room so men could sleep on one side of the room and women on the other. (Courtesy of David C. Lott.)

A group of visitors and local residents gathers on the front steps of the Medicine Park Clubhouse. The views from atop Mount Dunbar, where the clubhouse was located, were some of the best in the area. (Courtesy of Museum of the Great Plains.)

This photograph was taken in the spring of 1909. The following offers a glimpse at the economy of the period: In 1909, some 14 percent of homes had a bathtub; 8 percent of homes had a telephone; there were 8,000 cars and 144 miles of paved roads in America; the speed limit in most cities was 10 mph; the average wage was 22¢ per hour; sugar cost 4¢ a pound; eggs were 14¢ a dozen; coffee was 15¢ a pound; the average worker made between $200 and $400 per year, and there were about 230 reported murders in the country. Approximately 95 percent of today's taxes did not exist in 1909. (Courtesy of Bill Patty.)

In 1910, the Outside Inn was a large, roofed, open-air pavilion that featured dining tables and chairs inside. It had oak tree trunk support columns on all four sides of the building and a spacious front porch. The inn even had its own dairy and irrigated vegetable gardens. The basic structure still exists today as the single-story portion of the Old Plantation Restaurant. (Courtesy of Museum of the Great Plains.)

Pictured is the veranda style front porch of the Outside Inn about 1910. Note the timber support columns and the drawstring and roll-down canvas awning blinds along the top of the "windows." They were used to close off the pavilion or provide shade. (Courtesy of Museum of the Great Plains.)

This 1910 photograph features the interior of the Outside Inn. There were numerous dining tables and chairs for guests, and oil lanterns for lighting hung from the ceiling. Note the roll-down canvas awning blinds along the top of the "windows." (Courtesy of Museum of the Great Plains.)

Medicine Park founder Elmer Thomas and his partner, Hal Lloyd, originally formed Lawton Rapid Transit Railroad Company to own, manage, and promote the resort. They had proposed a rail system that would carry passengers the 15 or so miles from Lawton to Medicine Park in just 40 minutes. It never materialized as a railroad as envisioned, and instead they provided small open air "buses." The fare was $1 each way and 50¢ for trunks. Visitors flocked to the area to enjoy the mountains, swimming, and food. In the photograph above, Elmer Thomas and unknown guests enter the resort property through the eastern gateway. In the photograph below, a group of tourists boards the bus in front of the Outside Inn for their trip back into Lawton. Note the "bend twig" sign above the Inn's entry that spells out "Outside Inn." (Above, courtesy of David C. Lott; below, courtesy of Museum of the Great Plains.)

In this 1911 photograph, a group from the Pioneer Telephone Company poses on the rocks overlooking Bath Lake swimming hole on Medicine Creek. Note the small cabins dotting the hillside in the upper right. (Courtesy of Phyllis Young.)

In this 1912 photograph, a visitor to Medicine Park is featured standing with his prized 1912 Hupmobile. The Hupp Motor Company of Detroit started building automobiles in 1908 and introduced their creation, called the Model 20, to the public at the Detroit Auto Show in 1909; it was sold until 1940. The company's philosophy was to build a car in the workingman's price range. (Courtesy of Phyllis Young.)

It was a good day for fishing in Gondola Lake on Medicine Creek. In this 1912 photograph taken in front of the Outside Inn, a group of happy visitors proudly displays their day's catch. (Courtesy of Museum of the Great Plains.)

A brave diver in 1912 balances himself on the granite rocks as he prepares to take a plunge into Bath Lake. Note the bathhouse in the background and swimmers in the swimming hole. (Courtesy of Medicine Park Telephone Company.)

Two young ladies pose for a 1914 photograph in front of the bathhouse on the steps leading to the slide that would soon swoop them into the cool waters of Bath Lake. (Courtesy of Hank Sabine.)

A group of young people in 1914 swims near the base and pose on a diving platform built onto a large, submerged tree in the middle of Bath Lake swimming hole. (Courtesy of Phyllis Young.)

In 1914, Medicine Park was sold to D. L. Sleeper and Associates of Oklahoma City for $16,000. His group enclosed the Outside Inn and added a flat-roofed, wood-framed, two-story hotel. Cobblestone support columns replaced the tree trunk columns. In this photograph, one can see evidence of construction underway. D. L. Sleeper and Associates defaulted on the loan in 1915, and Thomas and Lloyd once again had possession of Medicine Park. (Courtesy of Bill Whitworth.)

In this 1915 photograph taken along East Lake Drive in Medicine Park, one can see a few of the cottages and cabins that were constructed as weekend and sometimes summer homes. Many of the dwellings had screened in sleeping porches that took advantage of cool summer breezes. Note the canvas awning that provided shade on the cabin and the Medicine Park Clubhouse atop Mount Dunbar. (Courtesy of Museum of the Great Plains.)

By 1915, there were numerous cabins dotting the hillsides and valleys of Medicine Park. A trend was begun to name individual cabins, such as "The Alpha," pictured above in this grouping of cabins along West Lake Drive. Most cabins were built using the cannonball-sized granite cobblestones that were such an abundant natural resource for the area. The cobblestones were formed millions of years through what geologists call the "freeze, thaw, tumble" process. (Courtesy of Medicine Park Telephone Company.)

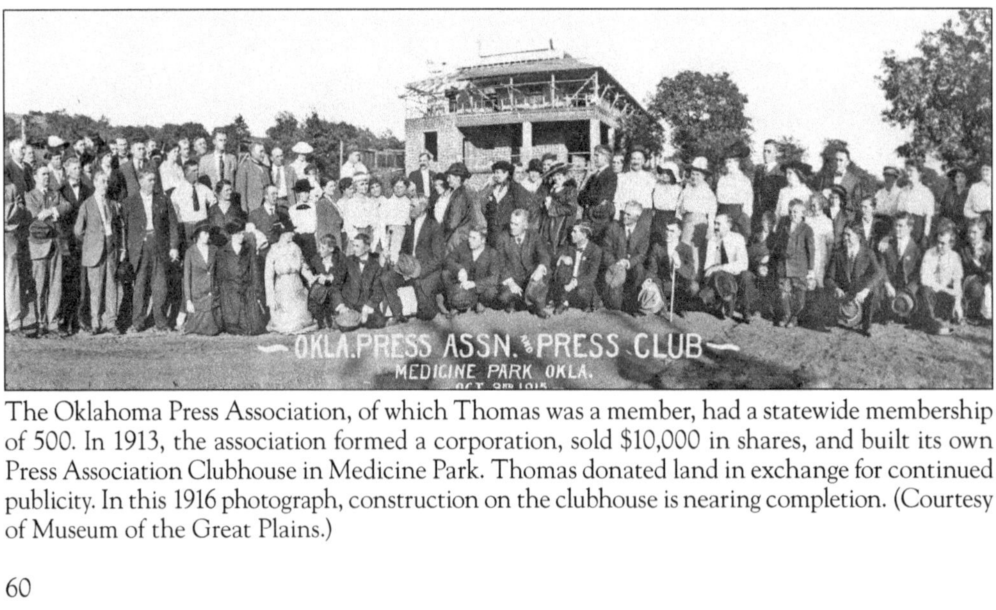


The Oklahoma Press Association, of which Thomas was a member, had a statewide membership of 500. In 1913, the association formed a corporation, sold $10,000 in shares, and built its own Press Association Clubhouse in Medicine Park. Thomas donated land in exchange for continued publicity. In this 1916 photograph, construction on the clubhouse is nearing completion. (Courtesy of Museum of the Great Plains.)

The Oklahoma Press Association Clubhouse opened April 24, 1916. The ground floor was used as a social area, and the second floor was equipped with cots and bedding. Lodging was available for members only. Men slept on one side of the hall, women on the other. (Courtesy of David and Candace McCoy.)

A visitor to Medicine Park in 1918 stands in front of the entry sign to the Oklahoma State Fish Hatchery. The state of Oklahoma's first such fish hatchery was constructed on land once homesteaded by Thomas, then donated to the state. It was built using prison labor in 1917. It serviced the Oklahoma Fish and Game Department's needs for stocking of lakes and farm ponds. (Courtesy of Museum of the Great Plains.)

The fountain and playground pictured in this 1918 photograph were on East Lake Drive, due east of the hotel. Cabins and cottages dot the hillside south of Medicine Creek. The playground became clay surface tennis courts in 1922. (Courtesy of Bill Patty.)

The water well in this 1918 photograph was on the northern bank of Medicine Creek, near Bath Lake and called "the springhouse." It later served as a bait house and part of a small zoo. In the course of excavation of the site for restoration late 2009, workers found a deeply buried water line. On it was a hidden turn valve tapped into one of Lawton's water mains. There was never actually an active spring. (Courtesy of Museum of the Great Plains.)

A pretty, young visitor to Medicine Park poses on the running board of an automobile in 1918. (Courtesy of Hank Sabine.)

Fishing in 1918 was often very good on Lake La-ton-ka, near Medicine Park, as is evidenced by this catch of several hundred pounds of catfish hauled in by these unknown fishermen. (Courtesy of Bill Whitworth.)

Medicine Park visitors in 1918 pose for a photograph on a portion of Bath Lake Dam on Medicine Creek. (Courtesy of Bill Whitworth.)

In this 1919 photograph is the Swinging Bridge across Medicine Creek, just on the west end of Bath Lake swimming hole. It provided not only foot traffic access to both sides of the creek, but also served as a good spot for people watching. It was also great fun to "rock the bridge" and get it to swing. Note the heavy timber support pylons set on each creek bank to provide support for the bridge. These were later replaced with massive concrete pylons. (Courtesy of Medicine Park Telephone Company.)

A two-story annex was built in 1916 adjacent to the hotel. The first floor, constructed with a facade of cobblestones, was called The Park Store and was operated by Edith Thomas. The second floor was wood-framed and served as additional hotel rooms, connected to the main hotel by a breezeway. This 1919 photograph shows the colorful awnings used as exterior window treatments. (Courtesy of Museum of the Great Plains.)

Thomas became the sole proprietor of Medicine Park when he bought Lloyd's interest in 1920. He changed the name of his company to the Medicine Park Company, and made numerous improvements to the hotel and Medicine Park. Cobblestone walls helped form terraces and gardens along the creek side of Bath Lake. The entire area had a beautiful gardenlike setting. Columns made of cobblestones that had electric street lamp were often constructed into the walls, as in this 1920 photograph. (Courtesy of Kenneth and Dora Hilliary.)

By 1920, Medicine Park was a full-blown resort community, just as Elmer Thomas had envisioned. Visitors from all around Oklahoma and northern Texas frequented the resort and enjoyed its park-like setting, activities, and hospitality. An article in the *Lawton Constitution* newspaper stated that more than 200,000 people visited Medicine Park in 1922, more than half coming from Texas. There were dozens of small rental cabins dotting the hillsides to the east of the hotel. Most of these cabins were constructed with facades of cobblestone and had screened-in sleeping porches, as well as small kitchens and bedding. (Above, courtesy of David C. Lott; below, courtesy of Medicine Park Telephone Company.)

In the mid-1920s, Parmenter's Apartments (upper right) were built on West Lake Drive, directly across from Bath Lake Dam, offering an alternative to cabin or lodge rental. (Courtesy of Bill Patty.)

This 1920 postcard shows just how much the Bath Lake swimming hole had developed and how popular the resort had become, as literally hundreds of people enjoy their day in Medicine Park. (Courtesy of Bill Patty.)

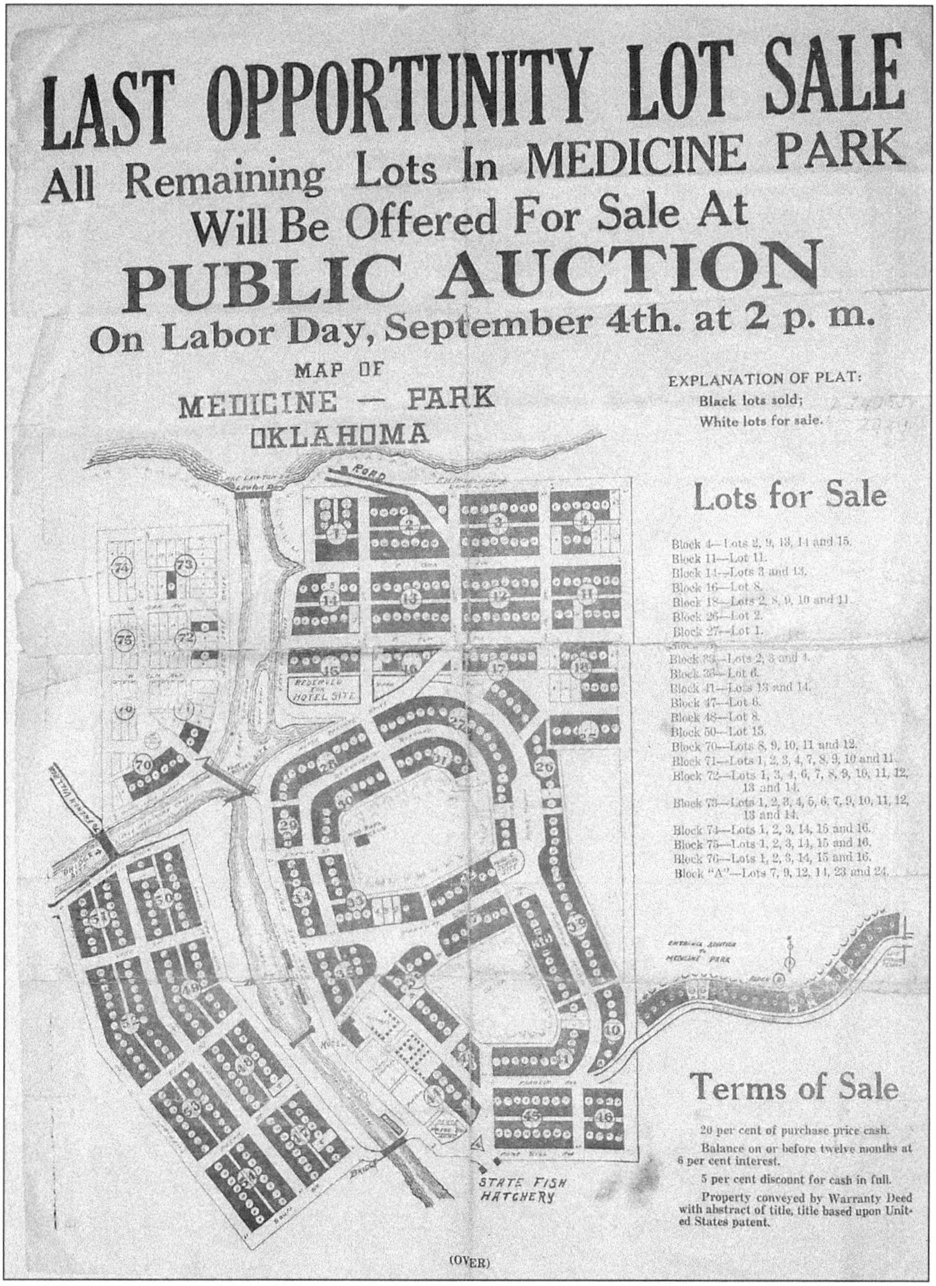


In the fall of 1921, Capt. Frank King was hired to resurvey the park and prepare for a public auction to sell remaining lots. A year later, this full-page advertisement began appearing in Lawton and surrounding area newspapers. This 1922 ad noted that on Labor Day, Monday, September 4, some 104 lots were to be sold at auction. On the plat drawing, black lots were already sold and white lots were those for sale. Terms of sale were "20 per cent of purchase price in cash; Balance on or before 12 months at 6 per cent interest; 5 per cent discount for cash in full; Property conveyed by Warranty Deed with abstract of title, title based upon United States patent." Of interest is that in the plat, a portion of the current site of Lawton's Water Treatment Plant was reserved as a hotel site. (Courtesy of Museum of the Great Plains.)

This 1922 flyer advertised the coming auction of remaining lots. All lots were 50-feet-by-140-feet. The flyer states that some lots had sold for as little as $16. The average lot sale was $60. All money from the sale was to be spent for bridges, roads, and improvements. The flyer also states "most of them are near American Legion French Village Colony donated to the boys." This evidently references a plan to build a home for veterans of World War I that never materialized. (Courtesy of Museum of the Great Plains.)

As the community grew, more residents became permanent, and a school was needed. In 1922, Thomas donated materials, labor, and land a block northwest of the hotel for a one-room schoolhouse in 1922. The schoolhouse is depicted in this photograph in the background behind the hotel. There were two outhouses near the school building, one for boys and one for girls. (Courtesy of David C. Lott.)

In this 1922 photograph taken from a hilltop on the southwestern edge of Medicine Park looking to the northeast, one can see the growth of the overall resort. The large building to the mid-right is the Oklahoma Press Association Clubhouse. (Courtesy of Bill Patty.)

Dr. C. W. Baird, a general practitioner and award-winning tennis player, built Baird's Sanatorium and Health Clinic at Thomas's request in 1922. It was located creek-side, across from the hotel and east of the present-day town hall. The large wooden structure featured his residence, Turkish baths, and a health clinic. There were also clay tennis courts across the street and east of the hotel. Baird was instrumental in getting state tennis tournaments held in Medicine Park. The spa was liberally patronized by visiting political associates of Senator Thomas. Many lively political discussions were held, and the upper floor was nicknamed the "Little White House." (Above, courtesy Medicine Park Telephone Company; below, courtesy the Leath family.)

By 1923, the resort featured a beautifully landscaped Bath Lake swimming area, the hotel and annex connected by a breezeway, and the Park Store. Other improvements included concessions, an enlarged bathhouse, and slides. There were rental cabins, summer homes, and permanent private residences throughout the community. Medicine Park was known as "The Jewel of the Southwest." (Courtesy of Medicine Park Telephone Company.)

After Elmer Thomas became the sole proprietor of Medicine Park in 1920, he made numerous improvements to the hotel, Bath Lake area, and throughout the resort. He built a spacious dance hall on the creek bank near the swinging bridge. This 1923 photograph shows that its construction was somewhat open-air, with wood-framed openings. Canvas tarps could be rolled down to close it off, and wooden shutters were later added. He also erected a checkered roofed arcade and several concessions structures. The Medicine Park Clubhouse, perched atop Mount Dunbar, provided limited lodging. (Courtesy of David C. Lott.)

These 1923 postcards show the popularity of the Bath Lake area. Visitors flocked to the resort in droves from all around the state of Oklahoma and north Texas to enjoy the cool waters, natural setting, entertainment and lodging. In the photograph above, visitors lined up on and near the swinging bridge to "people watch" and enjoy the views. The checkered roof arcade provided small carnival-like games of chance and fun, a small novelty photography studio, and a curio shop. The photograph below shows the bathhouse, hotel, and another view of the swimming hole. (Both courtesy of Bill Whitworth.)

In the mid-1920s, an unidentified professional photographer had a small studio inside the arcade near the dance hall. He had an assortment of costumes and a small variety of backdrops that patrons could use for creating novelty photographs and postcards. In the top photograph a young woman is posed as a cowgirl, complete with six-shooter, in front of a painted backdrop depicting the Bath Lake bathhouse. The term on the sign "A Bully Time" refers to terminology coined by former Pres. Teddy Roosevelt, who famously used the word bully to mean "superb" or "wonderful." In the bottom photograph, two unidentified young children are posed on a prop depicting a crescent moon, and the phrase "bully time" is used once again. (Both courtesy of Hank Sabine.)

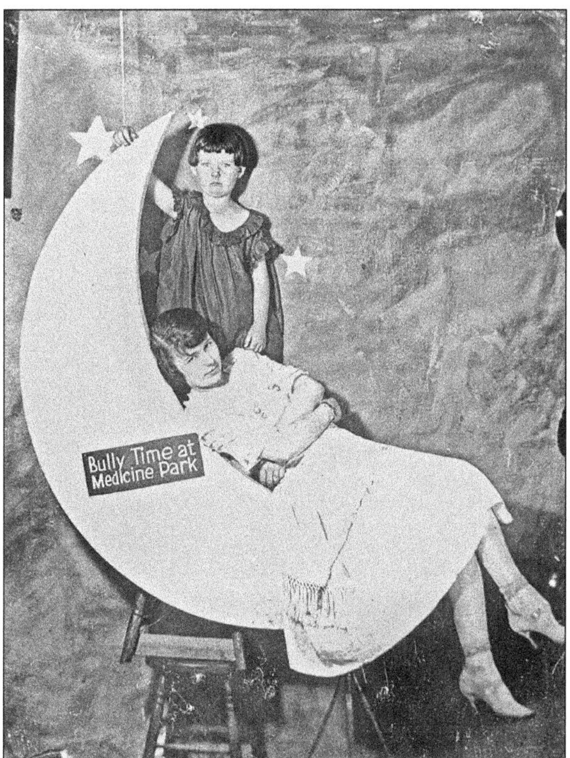

In 1925, Elmer Thomas added a third floor to the hotel and made numerous improvements to the building. The Outside Inn now boasted 50 rooms, an enlarged restaurant dining area, and 35 rental cabins. (Courtesy of Medicine Park Telephone Company.)

In the late spring of 1926, Medicine Creek flooded, washing out and damaging many structures along the creek, including the swinging bridge, which was rebuilt with reinforced concrete pylons in place of the original heavy wooden beam supports. It remained a popular vantage point for people watching at Bath Lake. (Courtesy of Medicine Park Telephone Company.)

On Easter Sunday, April 4, 1926, Lawton's Congregational Church members, with Rev. Anthony Mark Wallock (above), staged a passion play on a hilltop on the eastern edge of Medicine Park. That first play drew 200 visitors, growing to 500 the next year. In 1930, approximately 6,000 people witnessed Medicine Park's Easter pageant. In bottom photograph, cast members in the play portray angels gathered near the cross following the crucifixion scene. (Both courtesy of Museum of Great Plains.)

Fishing for bass, crappie, and catfish on Gondola Lake below Lake La-ton-ka was always a popular activity for visitors to Medicine Park. For those who wanted to cool off and people watch, Bath Lake was the place to be. (Above, courtesy of David C. Lott; below, courtesy of Museum of the Great Plains.)

# *Seven*

# The Depression and World War II Era

In the spring of 1926, Medicine Creek flooded and washed out many structures, including the bathhouse, auto bridge, and creek-side dance hall. Soon all were rebuilt. That same year, Thomas sold Medicine Park to a corporation of doctors, who changed the hotel's name to the Grand Hotel. Their era is filled with legends of gambling, slot machines, bootleg whiskey, and "pretty girls."

Medicine Park was operated by the doctors' corporation until 1939, when Lulabelle Young (later Hutchins) bought 360 acres of the venture. The hotel, which had been used primarily as a tax shelter, was in a dilapidated state. She refurbished it in the latest fashion with red tufted and draped ceilings and murals painted by Oklahoma artist Don Blanding. She also added a stone bar 60 feet in length. Even through World War II, the resort's economy thrived under Lulabelle's guidance. She put people to work during tough times, paying them $1 a day plus meals. She tiled the floors of 30 cabins, expanded the bathhouse to include shops and an arcade, and built a new swinging bridge and a 110-foot slide. She also added a small zoo and converted the dance hall into a skating rink. The drawing card became weekend dances. On special occasions, big dances were staged in the skating rink. Famous bands of the era, such as Pinky Tomblin, Les Brown, and Bob Wills and Texas Playboys delighted audiences.

Following the end of World War II, Lulabelle sold her property three times—always having to take possession again after the new owners defaulted. The third story of the hotel and the second story of the annex burned while under ownership of one of the groups. Lulabelle finally sold the property in 1954 to the Texas Land Company. The transaction was made in part by her trading for land in Texas. They operated as a resort for a while, but times were changing as the urbanization of America began. The company rented parts of the hotel and other properties, including the skating rink, to various businesspeople after 1955. The glory days of Medicine Park as a resort seemed to be fading.

In 1926, Thomas sold a large part of what was left of his holdings in Medicine Park to a corporation of doctors. During this period, however, the park underwent a transformation away from its original family recreation and pleasure resort. Their era is filled with legends of widespread gambling, slot machines, bootlegged whiskey, and women. This transition did not please Senator Thomas. In this mid-spring 1926 photograph, it is evident that Bath Lake is still a popular attraction. However, the Medicine Park Clubhouse atop Mount Dunbar had burned and is in a dilapidated state. (Courtesy of Museum of the Great Plains.)

Unidentified visitors to Medicine Park pose for a photograph in 1927 outside of the Medicine Park Post Office, which was between the Park Store and the residence of Sen. Elmer Thomas. (Courtesy of Glenda Turner.)

By July 1930, the Press Association was having difficulty funding its clubhouse and sold it for $4,000. The association's directors "believed it had served its usefulness to the association." It was purchased by the Hutchins family of Lawton, who leased it to Frank Wright. He converted it into the Apache Inn, complete with an elaborate dining area and sleeping rooms. (Courtesy of David and Candace McCoy.)

In this 1932 photograph of the refurbished Apache Inn, Fort Sill officers mount their horses and prepare their dogs for a foxhunt. (Courtesy of David C. Lott.)

The Apache Inn proved to be quite successful. In this mid-1930s photograph, a group enjoys a banquet hosted by Henry G. Bennett, president of Oklahoma A&M College (now OSU) from 1928 until 1950. In 1950, President Truman appointed Dr. Bennett to assistant secretary of state in charge of the Point Four Program to assist underdeveloped countries. He established more than 105 projects in 33 nations. Dr. Bennett and his wife died in a plane crash in Iran in 1950. The Point Four Program evolved into the U.S. Agency for International Development (USAID). The Apache Inn burned down in 1939. (Courtesy of Museum of the Great Plains.)

Following the flood of Medicine Creek in the late spring of 1926, the considerably damaged dance hall was rebuilt. In this 1930 photograph, the building now features a series of steel tubular supports and a rounded metal roofline, as it still does to this day. (Courtesy of David C. Lott.)

Due to the growing popularity of the Easter pageant, in 1934–1935 the Works Progress Administration (WPA) built the present-day Holy City of the Wichitas in the refuge, 5 miles west of its original location in Medicine Park. A $94,000 federal grant authorized by President Roosevelt supported construction of the outdoor amphitheater and numerous granite structures intended to recreate the Holy Land and serve as a setting for the annual passion play. (Courtesy of Kenneth and Dora Hilliary.)

The Holy City's non-denominational "World Chapel," as Reverend Wallock called it, is constructed of various sizes of native granite rock. In some cases, the rocks are basketball-sized, and in others they weigh up to several hundred pounds. The chapel features twin towers and a large open room for services. It is and has always been available for public use for such functions as weddings, funeral services, special church services, and meetings. (Courtesy of Kenneth and Dora Hilliary.)

The interior of the chapel features an elaborately painted ceiling and numerous works of art conceived and painted by Irene Malcolm of Lawton. She was called "the Michelangelo of the Wichitas," and her works of art took several years to complete. (Courtesy of David C. Lott.)

Around 1935, a small hydroelectric generating station was built on Gondola Dam on Medicine Creek to help provide electricity to the resort of Medicine Park and the fish hatchery. It was constructed and owned by Wolverton Electric Company. In addition, a transmission line was constructed from Medicine Park to the Holy City to provide electricity to power the lighting used during the Easter pageant. (Courtesy of Bill Whitworth.)

The Lone Oak Cottages in the late 1930s were a grouping of six cobblestone and wood-framed rentals along West Lake Drive. They were available to visitors for overnight, weekly, and even monthly rental. (Courtesy of David and Candace McCoy.)

Bob Wills and his Texas Playboys, the kings of western swing, became regulars at the Medicine Park Dance Hall from 1933 through the early 1940s. Western swing combined jazz, hillbilly, boogie, blues, big-band swing, rumba, mariachi and even jitterbug. By the mid-1940s, the Playboys were among the most versatile and innovative bands in America, with such songs as "Take Me Back to Tulsa" and "New San Antonio Rose." (Courtesy of Rosetta Wills.)

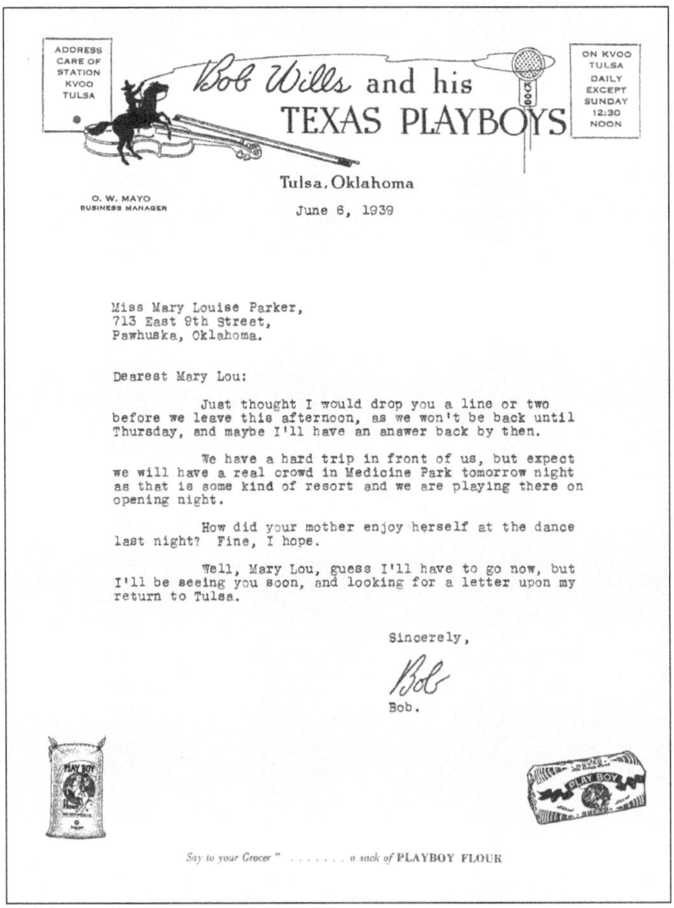

ADDRESS CARE OF STATION KVOO TULSA

Bob Wills and his TEXAS PLAYBOYS

ON KVOO TULSA DAILY EXCEPT SUNDAY 12:30 NOON

Tulsa, Oklahoma

O. W. MAYO
BUSINESS MANAGER

June 6, 1939

Miss Mary Louise Parker,
713 East 9th Street,
Pawhuska, Oklahoma.

Dearest Mary Lou:

Just thought I would drop you a line or two before we leave this afternoon, as we won't be back until Thursday, and maybe I'll have an answer back by then.

We have a hard trip in front of us, but expect we will have a real crowd in Medicine Park tomorrow night as that is some kind of resort and we are playing there on opening night.

How did your mother enjoy herself at the dance last night? Fine, I hope.

Well, Mary Lou, guess I'll have to go now, but I'll be seeing you soon, and looking for a letter upon my return to Tulsa.

Sincerely,

Bob

Bob.

Say to your Grocer " . . . . . . . a sack of PLAYBOY FLOUR

In this June 1939 letter, Bob Wills speaks to Mary Louise Parker of Pawhuska of "having a real crowd in Medicine Park tomorrow night." In his letter, he hopes upon his return to Tulsa "maybe I'll have an answer back by then." She said yes, and they were married on July 22, 1939. On November 8, 1939, their marriage was annulled. A few months later, upon learning Mary Lou was pregnant, Wills had the annulment set aside. They remained married for 13 months, after their daughter, Rosetta, was born, but the marriage ended on June 3, 1941. (Courtesy of David C. Lott.)

The Medicine Park Post Office was first established in October 1908. For several years it was located in the Outside Inn. In 1917, it was moved to a small cobblestone building constructed between the Elmer Thomas home and the Park Store. In this late-1930s photograph are pictured Edward "Junior" Hilliary (left) and his brother, Kenneth. (Courtesy of Kenneth and Dora Hilliary Collection.)

Lulabelle Young, pictured in this rare 1940 photograph, bought the Medicine Park land holdings, comprising some 360 acres, from the doctors' corporation in 1939. They had operated it primarily as a tax shelter since 1926. She stated, "I wanted to be the only woman to own a town. I bought it for the glory of it." She and her two children lived in a suite in the hotel's annex. She later became Lulabelle Hutchins after marrying Bob Hutchins. (Courtesy of David C. Lott.)

The lobby of the renamed Medicine Park Lodge was redecorated in 1940 by Lulabelle, as were the dining room and the "Silver Lounge," with its 60-foot long stone bar, tufted draped ceilings, and murals painted by Don Blanding, an Oklahoma artist. She also added a stone guest check-in counter in the hotel lobby. (Courtesy of Museum of the Great Plains.)

Lulabelle made numerous improvements to the Bath Lake swimming hole, the bathhouse, and the arcade area, which also featured food and beverage concessions. She also added a small zoo with monkeys and bears. (Courtesy of Kenneth and Dora Hilliary.)

Pictured here are the Park Store and Medicine Park Lodge annex during the period of Lulabelle Hutchins' ownership. The Park Store was a general merchandise store that sold food, beverages, curios, ice, and general dry goods. (Courtesy of Kenneth and Dora Hilliary.)

Sandwiched in between the Park Store and Elmer Thomas's home was the Medicine Park Post Office. It was just a very small cobblestone structure that contained a limited number of post office boxes and a counter for the postmaster. (Courtesy of Kenneth and Dora Hilliary.)

Lulabelle converted the dance hall into a skating rink in 1940. On special occasions, big dances drawing large crowds were staged in the skating rink. Numerous big bands made their way through Medicine Park in route to venues in Oklahoma City, Dallas, and Fort Worth. However, its mainstay was a skating rink, and Lulabelle hired Claude and Lois Thomas (no relation to Elmer Thomas) to manage the business around 1942. Skating parties were often held for visitors and residents of Medicine Park. (Courtesy of Glo King-Wiley.)

Claude and Lois Thomas purchased 27 rental cabins in the early 1940s. The couple named the assortment of cabins dotting the hillsides in various parts of town as "Merry Circle." This photograph is a professionally staged advertisement of a model "cowgirl" posing at the cobblestone entry gate to a grouping of Merry Circle Cabins. (Courtesy of Museum of the Great Plains.)

The Thomas family converted one of the cabins into the Merry Circle Grocery Store. The store was located at the main entry into town, one block east from the "S" curve leading into Medicine Park's town center. The small store served as a grocery store, meat market, deli, newsstand and office for cabin rental. (Courtesy of Glo King-Wiley.)

Claude and Lois Thomas are pictured at right sitting on a bench in front of the Merry Circle Grocery Store. (Courtesy of Glo King-Wiley.)

Each of the 27 Merry Circle cabins was named by a member of the Thomas family to give them their own identity. In this 1944 photograph are the Annie Morrow Cabin and the Blue Heaven Cabin. The cabins were available for rental by the night, weekend, week, or month. (Courtesy of Glo King-Wiley.)

This 1944 photograph shows the Billy Cabin in the main grouping of cabins called Merry Circle. It is a long, narrow shotgun-style cobblestone structure located on Longhorn Street behind the Merry Circle Grocery Store. (Courtesy of Glo King-Wiley.)

The Will Rogers Cabin was one of the largest at Merry Circle. It is a two-story wood-framed home built atop a cobblestone-lined concrete foundation. The home features numerous beautiful windows on all sides. The restored home is located on the corner of Longhorn and Buffalo Streets one block behind the Merry Circle Store, next door to the Billy Cabin. (Courtesy of Glo King-Wiley.)

This late-1930s photograph shows five cobblestone cabins along East Lake Drive in the town center of Medicine Park. A few years later they would become a part of the Merry Circle Cabins operation owned by Claude and Lois Thomas. Today the cabins are all little shops and galleries. In the far right is the roofline of Baird's Sanitarium, which burned to the ground in about 1939. (Courtesy of Glo King-Wiley.)

In this photograph are Patrica Thomas King and husband Kenneth King in front of the Merry Circle Store. Patrica was the daughter of Claude and Lois Thomas. The Kings owned and operated Merry Circle from 1947 into the late 1970s. (Courtesy of Glo King-Wiley.)

A customer stands at the counter inside of Merry Circle Store owned and operated by Patrica and Kenneth King. (Courtesy of Glo King-Wiley.)

Kenneth King stands in the doorway of Lady Alice Cabin (1 of 27 cabins owned by the Kings), two houses down from Merry Circle Grocery Store. (Courtesy of Glo King-Wiley.)

A young Claude Owen King catches up on his comic book reading at the newsstand located inside Merry Circle Grocery Store in the early 1950s. (Courtesy of Glo King-Wiley.)

Around 1951, a car careened off the road and ran into the gas pumps in front of the original cobblestone structure that housed Merry Circle Grocery Store. The resulting explosion not only killed the driver, but also burned the store to the ground. The store was rebuilt using cinder blocks and enlarged to more than triple the original floor space. Merry Circle Grocery Store continued to operate until 1989. (Courtesy of Glo King-Wiley.)

In 1948, Hollywood came to the Holy City of the Wichitas and filmed a full-color, feature-length movie titled *The Lawton Story of The Prince of Peace.* The film was produced by Kroger Babb and J. S. Josey of Hallmark Productions (no relation to Hallmark Cards) and was directed by William Beaudine and Harold Daniels. Much of the film was shot on location at The Holy City and at various locations in Lawton, and portions were filmed at Hal Roach Studios in Culver City, California. The film starred a young Ginger Prince, who was being billed as the next Shirley Temple, as well as Forrest Taylor, Millard Coody, Darlene Bridges, and a cast of 3,000 from the local area and 32 states. The film told the story of the Holy City's founder Rev. Mark Wallock, played by Forrest Taylor, and the world famous Easter pageant. At the world premiere in Lawton, seats went for as much as $1,000. Producer Kroger Babb was a master at "ballyhoo" and public relations hype. The film received international recognition and played throughout the United States, Canada, and even Mexico and other international locations for the next five years. (Courtesy of David C. Lott.)

The old bathhouse on Medicine Creek's Bath Lake had an arcade on its north side, facing East Lake Drive. It contained around a half-dozen small businesses—two of which (Foxie Dogs and Hamburgers and a soda and ice cream stand) are depicted in this late-1940s photograph. Grundy made refers to with all the condiments. (Courtesy of Medicine Park Telephone Company.)

The Medicine Park Lodge was starting to lose a bit of its luster by the late 1940s. The urbanization of America was beginning its boom time, and rural areas and resorts began paying the price across the country as interest declined. Medicine Park simply followed that trend. (Courtesy of Glo King-Wiley.)

The Medicine Park Fish Hatchery, operated by the Oklahoma Fish and Game Department, sits on land originally homesteaded by Elmer Thomas in 1901. In 1912, he donated 10 acres to the state, and the state bought an additional 10 acres. A bordering section of land was also acquired. Built using prison labor, the hatchery opened in 1915. In 1918, an 8-inch water line from Lake La-ton-ka Dam was built to provide water for the hatchery. By 1923, there were 12 ponds. In this late-1940s photograph, there are some 40 cells. (Courtesy of Oklahoma Department of Wildlife Conservation.)

In December 1923, James Arthur Manning went to work for the Oklahoma Fish and Game Department at the Medicine Park Fish Hatchery for $60 a month. The superintendent at that time was Carl McDonald. Manning became the hatchery's superintendent in 1928, and he served as such until 1961. This late-1940s photograph shows Manning with a hatchery-raised catfish. In 1987, the Oklahoma Wildlife Conservation Commission officially renamed the operation as James Arthur Manning Fish Hatchery to honor his service. (Courtesy of Oklahoma Department of Wildlife Conservation.)

This photograph shows one of the many ponds at the James Arthur Manning Fish Hatchery in Medicine Park. In addition to raising bass, crappie, and catfish to meet the growing demand from farm ponds across the state, the facility also featured a number of flower gardens, and the area was stocked with deer, elk, buffalo, pheasant, quail, and wild turkey. (Courtesy of Kenneth and Dora Hilliary.)

The superintendent's home at the fish hatchery, seen in this 1948 photograph, was originally built just prior to 1920. It was in later years simply called the Manning House. For many years prior to and during the 1920s, the only telephones in the area were at the fish hatchery and the Park Store in the town center of Medicine Park. Following Manning's retirement in the early 1960s, the house became dilapidated, and the state decided not to spend the money to restore it. It was torn down in 2008. (Courtesy of Oklahoma Department of Wildlife Conservation.)

# *Eight*

# Early 1950s and Becoming a Town

Following World War II, the urbanization of America began. In the early 1950s, large populations shifted from rural areas to the cities, encouraged by expectations for an improved standard of living, jobs, and new housing construction. Rural resorts across the nation experienced sharp decline as people found entertainment and recreation in urban areas. As a resort, Medicine Park's decline was characteristic of the times.

From the mid-1940s through the 1960s, several commercial properties were sold to individuals. The town experienced a wide variety of social and economic struggles, and the late 1940s began a period of decline for Medicine Park as a resort. It had evolved itself more into a town than a resort.

From 1942 through the 1970s, Medicine Park had numerous small businesses. They included the Dam Café, Merry Circle Cabins and Grocery Store, Callaway's Grocery and Market, Medicine Park Service Station, Cecil's Beauty Shop, Medicine Park Café, Carpenter's Grocery (later Haile's Grocery), Beasley's Wichita Mountains Service Station, and an assortment of taverns and drinking establishments.

The hotel, still owned by Texas Land Company, was closed for a number of years until 1966, when it was leased to Rex and Ruby "Grandma" Leath. The couple set up an antique shop and began living in the hotel. In 1973, they purchased the building, renaming it the Old Plantation Restaurant. It was listed as The Medicine Park Hotel on the National Register of Historic Places on September 28, 1979.

In 1968, the Comanche County Commissioners were petitioned by residents for an election to allow a vote on incorporating Medicine Park as an Oklahoma town. This action was needed to create a governmental structure that would be able to qualify for federal grants and loans and generate revenue for loan repayment. The top priority was construction of a municipal sewer collection and treatment system that would eliminate the flow of raw sewage into Medicine Creek. After a successful election effort, the new town was incorporated as the town of Medicine Park by the Board of Comanche County Commissioners on July 30, 1969.

The first school classes in Medicine Park (1916–1921) were taught by Leona Hilliary in a tiny cobblestone building adjacent to the Park Store and hotel. In 1921, Elmer Thomas donated land and provided the materials and labor to build a new, larger school about a block northwest of the hotel. By 1926, a still larger school was needed, so Thomas once again donated land, materials, and labor for a new school. This late-1940s photograph is of one of the Medicine Park School buildings located on West Lake Drive. It later had a brick facade and cedar added to the building. A couple of years later, Thomas built a cobblestone auditorium, and in later years, other structures were built nearby, including a gymnasium and small lunchroom. The school provided classes for children first through eighth grades. The school closed in the early 1990s, and classes were absorbed into the Lawton and Elgin school district. (Courtesy of Judy Robertson.)

This 1950 photograph shows a cobblestone home located across the street from the Medicine Park School on West Lake Drive. (Courtesy of Judy Robertson.)

The Bath Lake swimming hole on Medicine Creek remained a popular attraction for Medicine Park well into the 1950s and early 1960s. In this 1950 photograph, a young diver contemplates his dive into the waters. The bathhouse and its nearby slides remained operational until a fire destroyed the bathhouse in 1964. (Courtesy of David and Candace McCoy.)

The rock island outcropping in Bath Lake was always a popular spot to enter the waters. This 1950 photograph depicts an "umbrella" shower. Water was pumped from the creek up through the column and it showered down atop the umbrella to cool or rinse off the visitors. (Courtesy of David and Candace McCoy.)

Shown to the left are several people watching their children swim in the waters of Bath Lake near the footbridge that led out onto the rock island outcropping. (Courtesy of David and Candace McCoy.)

The skating rink was still a popular attraction for Medicine Park in 1950. First built in 1920 as a dance hall, the original structure was heavily damaged in the flood of 1926. It was rebuilt with tubular steel half-circle support framing and a rounded metal roofline like one would find on an airplane hanger. There were shutters on three sides that opened up to provide air circulation. (Courtesy of David and Candace McCoy.)

In these 1950 photographs are depicted the Dam Cafe. The cafe with the humorous name was located near the Lake Lawtonka Dam in the late 1940s and early 1950s. They served hamburgers, sandwiches, plate lunches, sodas, much coffee, and homemade pies. The cafe also sold bait and a limited amount of fishing tackle. It was a favorite hangout for fishermen, visitors, and local residents who fished on Gondola Lake, Lake Lawtonka, or below the dam. (Above, courtesy of Kenneth and Dora Hilliary; below, courtesy of Museum of the Great Plains.)

Pictured here are the Grand Hotel, Park Store, and apartments in Medicine Park about the time they were purchased from Lulabelle Hutchins by Texas Land Company in 1954. The new owners soon changed the name of the hotel to simply the Medicine Park Hotel. (Courtesy of David and Candace McCoy.)

Sandy Davis, daughter of Curtis and June Davis of Texas Land Company, and the sister of Candace (Davis) McCoy, enjoys her afternoon motoring her tricycle down the large porch in front of the hotel in this *c.* 1955 photograph. (Courtesy of David and Candace McCoy.)

Callaway's Grocery and Market, located on Forrest Street was in operation in Medicine Park from 1947 to 1968. The small family-run store sold basic grocery items such as canned goods, fruits and vegetables, meats, dairy products, beverages, ice, and cold beer. The store was owned and operated by Marion "M. J." and Ovelda Callaway. (Courtesy of Marilyn Callaway Cosgrove.)

Medicine Park residents, from left to right, an unidentified boy, Johnny Nix, another unidentified youth, and Lon Billeau and their horses always enjoyed a brief stop at Callaway's Store for a little refreshment. (Courtesy of Marilyn Callaway Cosgrove.)

M. J. Callaway wrestles a block of ice from the ice dock at Callaway's Grocery and Market in this mid-1950s photograph. (Courtesy of Marilyn Callaway Cosgrove.)

Ovelda Callaway poses for a mid-1950s photograph near the store's magazine rack and merchandising display of Schlitz beer, advertising the new half-quart can. (Courtesy of Marilyn Callaway Cosgrove.)

Callaway's Grocery and Market had an on-premise consumption beer license as well as a carryout sales license. One of the regulars, John Eddie Pace, poses for this 1955 photograph with a beer in hand. From all reports, John Eddie was quite a colorful character, who wore heavy wool clothing year round. (Courtesy of Marilyn Callaway Cosgrove.)

Another legendary character in Medicine Park was Burl Alfon Haile. Born in 1902, Burl was always a sharp dresser and good storyteller. Legends have it that he was also quite crafty in a hearty game of cards. Burl passed away in 1999. (Courtesy of Jean Haile)

In the mid- to late 1950s, on Upper East Lake Drive, due north of the Music Hall, was Haile's Grocery Store. The small family-run store sold fresh meats, picnic supplies, film, candy, tobacco products, beverages, and basic grocery items. In this photograph are Rena Jo Burke (left), Van Aflon Haile (center), and Van Leon Haile. (Courtesy of Jean Haile)

This 1957 photograph depicts the Medicine Park Post Office and the Past Time Club, located in the former Park Store and hotel annex. The upper floor of the annex building had burned a few years before and was demolished. The club served cold pop and beer and sold film as well as picnic supplies. (Courtesy of David and Candace McCoy.)

This 1957 photograph is taken from the western porch of the hotel in Medicine Park. Upper East Lake Drive and East Lake Drive, just west of the hotel, has always been a busy spot for parking for easy access to the bathhouse, the arcade and Bath Lake swimming hole. The skating rink is seen on the far right. (Courtesy of David and Candace McCoy.)

Local musicians play on the small stage at the hotel in this *c.* 1957 photograph. (Courtesy of David and Candace McCoy.)

Ruth Witt, pictured in 1959, taught first and second grades at the Medicine Park School for many years. She was one of the students' favorite teachers. (Courtesy of Marilyn Callaway Cosgrove.)

Medicine Park School students pose for this 1966 photograph in front of the school's outdoor sign. (Courtesy of Melinda Freeman Whitewolf.)

Students in 1966 line up outside on the playground to enter the lunchroom and be served a hearty lunch at the Medicine Park School. At the time, the lunchroom was housed in a cobblestone building constructed in 1928 and was one of only two structures for the school. In 1926–1927, before the cobblestone lunchroom was built, students had to walk from the school, across the auto-bridge to the first in a grouping of small cobblestone structures used now for retail shops and galleries today. In later years, students had a small metal building next to the gymnasium that served as the lunchroom. (Courtesy of Melinda Freeman Whitewolf.)

Students enjoy a quick game of football on the playground at the Medicine Park School in this 1966 photograph. (Courtesy of Melinda Freeman Whitewolf.)

The Happy Hollow is shown here in this early-1960s photograph. It is located on State Highway 49 in Medicine Park near the main entry to the Wichita Mountains Wildlife Refuge. The store, still in existence today, sells curios, souvenirs, picnic items, soft drinks, and a variety of gift items. (Courtesy of Melinda Freeman Whitewolf.)

In 1966, Ruby "Grandma" Leath and her husband, Rex, leased the hotel, which had been closed for a number of years, from the Texas Land Company. Shortly thereafter, following cleaning the property up and hauling away haul away 50 bales of hay, 3 loads of sand and 30 loads of trash, the couple moved from Walters, set up an antique shop, and began living in a portion of the hotel. In 1973, the couple bought the hotel and renamed it the Old Plantation Restaurant. This photograph of Grandma was taken in 1969. (Courtesy of Museum of the Great Plains.)

In 1968, residents petitioned for an election to have Medicine Park incorporated so the town could qualify for government grants and loans to provide infrastructure improvements, and collect taxes. The town officially incorporated on July 30, 1969. Here, seven officials are sworn in as members of the town board of trustees by District Judge Toby Morris. They are, from left to right, Raymond C. Gardner, Claude T. Buffalo, Maynard J. Fuller Jr., Edward A. Hilliary, A. H. "Jack" Laughter, Troy H. Laird, and Roy Brown. Other early town officials included Rex Leath, "Doc" Dodson, and A. P. Tuck, who served as police commissioner. (Courtesy of Cecil Gardner.)

If the walls of the old Medicine Park Hotel could only talk, what tales they could tell. Grandma Leath liked to imagine what they could say, but since they didn't talk, she did the talking for them. She could always be found at an Old Plantation Restaurant's table spinning her yarns and tall tales of bygone days to whomever would listen. In this 1979 photograph, Grandma visits with Oklahoma governor George Nigh (far right), his wife, Donna Nigh, and an unidentified associate. (Courtesy of Rex and Ruby Leath family.)

Rex Leath could always be found behind the bar of the Old Plantation serving up cold beer and soda pop to customers, or being the cashier. He was known to spin a pretty good tale himself and always had a smile and a good joke to tell. The Medicine Park Hotel was placed on the National Register of Historic Places on September 28, 1979. (Courtesy of Rex and Ruby Leath family.)

Grandma Leath and the Old Plantation Restaurant were known for their burgers, catfish, huge 22-ounce sirloin steaks that "hung off the platter," cold beer, and famous, homemade hot rolls the size of a baseball. In this photograph, Grandma has just pulled a tray of her famous hot rolls out of the oven, ready to serve. (Courtesy of Museum of the Great Plains.)

# THE OLD PLANTATION
## RESTAURANT
### Medicine Park, Oklahoma
### GRANDMA'S HOMEMADE HOT ROLLS

| | |
|---|---|
| 1 EGG | 1/2 CUP SUGAR |
| 1 YEAST CAKE | 2 CUPS LUKE WARM WATER |
| 1 TSP. SALT | 7 CUPS FLOUR |

Mix above ingredients. Let rise to double size. Work down. Put in greased pan, let rise to double size. Cook in 400 degree oven until golden brown.

Phone 529-9641     Rex & Grandma • Owners

Grandma Leath was so proud of her hot rolls and the Old Plantation was so well known for them that she printed and distributed literally tens of thousands of cards that displayed the recipe for all to see. She was also known for making copies of news clippings and items of local history to distribute freely to customers who expressed an interest—and there was always a copy of the recipe card for the rolls attached. (Courtesy of David C. Lott.)

This is one of the last known professional photographs of Rex and Ruby "Grandma" Leath. The photograph was taken to commemorate the couple's 50th wedding anniversary. Rex passed away in the late 1990s, and Ruby passed away in 2007. (Courtesy of Museum of the Great Plains.)

Since incorporating as a town, the Medicine Park volunteer fire department and police department have periodically held fund-raisers as a means of assisting in operations of the vital community-based services. This early-1970s fund-raising poster was found by David Lott sandwiched inside a wall during restoration of the skating rink. It was later donated and sold at a benefit auction in Medicine Park to raise funds for an ailing local resident. (Courtesy of Dr. Kenneth Gunkel.)

Billy Arnold and the Branders was a top-notch band from late 1960s and early 1970s from Lawton. They played frequently in Medicine Park and throughout the region of southwest Oklahoma and north Texas. Pictured here are band members Karl Waldbauer (on the ground), Tommy Todd (on the stairs to the left), Mike Griffith (standing on the pipe at right), Chuck Caldwell (kneeling on stairs), and Billy Arnold (top of stairs). (Courtesy of Chris Caldwell.)

# *Nine*

# Medicine Park's Revitalization

The pattern of declining investment in Medicine Park turned around in the early 1990s. Edna Hennessee decided to bring her dormant Big Rock Mountain Estates housing development project back to life. She hired David Lott as project manager, and the property was resurveyed, engineered and platted. The project's first phase featured 180 custom homesites, and more than 7,200 feet of paved road.

In 1995, David and Candace McCoy purchased the Riverside Café. Candace, the daughter of Texas Land Company's principal Curtis Davis, was born in Medicine Park in 1954, at the time her parents operated the resort. The couple relocated to Medicine Park from McAllen, Texas, and restored the Riverside Café. After the cafe opened in 1996, new visitors began coming to town once again.

In 1997, David Lott purchased the skating rink, which had originally been built as a dance hall in 1920 before becoming a skating rink. Following extensive restoration, the Medicine Park Music Hall opened, providing live music shows and serving burgers, steaks, and barbeque. The hall hosted numerous concerts, including Michael Martin Murphy, Rare Earth, Canned Heat, Mitch Ryder and The Detroit Wheels, Lovin' Spoonful, Iron Butterfly, Dan Hicks and the Hot Licks, The Byrds, Leon Russell, Head East, Hank Thompson, Big Brother and the Holding Company, 1964-Beatles Tribute, Amazing Rhythm Aces, and more. In early 2002, short-term financing forced the business to close.

Public interest the music hall had generated provided a catalyst, bringing new businesses with other economic successes soon following. To date, numerous buildings have been restored, including the Old Plantation Restaurant and the Apache Inn. The town boasts 50 businesses, including a tavern, winery, gift shops, galleries, mixed-drinks club, a reopened music hall, ice cream parlor, fast-food restaurants, a variety store, travel stop, wedding chapel, and numerous cottages for tourist accommodations. In recent years, 30 new homes have been built in Medicine Park.

Medicine Park has grown into an arts community with several artists in residence, including sculptors, painters, graphic designers, Web designers, photographers, musicians, and street theater actors. From regular gallery openings at the Winery of the Wichitas, to special events in town, to bands playing on the lawn at the Park Tavern throughout the summer, spring, and fall, and trout fishing in the winter months, Medicine Park is a great place to visit any time. More information can be found at www.medicinepark.com.

Numerous residential structures in Medicine Park have been restored in recent years. Pictured here is the historic Sen. Elmer Thomas home on Upper East Lake Drive. Originally built in 1920, restoration on the home began in 1995 by Maredith Bomberger, the granddaughter of Elmer Thomas. She has since passed away, and the new owners have completed her efforts. (Courtesy of David C. Lott.)

Commercial properties, such as this grouping of five small cobblestone buildings in what is called the town center of Medicine Park, have also been restored. The retail businesses, ranging from gift shops, galleries, and gourmet food stores, are open each weekend and offer a variety of unique gift and personal items. (Courtesy of David C. Lott.)

For 100 years, Medicine Park has offered visitors unique opportunities for nightly, weekend, or weekly lodging. There are currently some 30 cabins, cottages, and bed and breakfast rooms available. In addition the Apache Inn has been rebuilt much as it was in the 1920s. In the picture above are two cobblestone cabins located in the town center of Medicine Park. They are called the Twins because not only are they next door to each other, they are also almost identical in size and floor plan. In the photograph below is the Medicine Park Cabin located on West Lake Drive. The cabin is known for the current owners' attention to detail and amenities offered to their guests. (Both courtesy of David C. Lott.)

New construction of homes in Medicine Park began in the mid-1990s with the revitalization of Edna Hennessee's Big Rock Mountain Estates. In this photograph is a two-story Western-style log home with a wonderful wraparound porch. (Courtesy of David C. Lott.)

The Granite Ridge addition, west of Gondola Lake in Medicine Park, began in 2007 and is known for its timeless classic design and arts and crafts period charm. David and Candace McCoy are home designers and builders who pay a great deal attention to quality and detail. (Courtesy of David C. Lott.)

About a dozen new homes have been built in the older sections of Medicine Park in recent years. The home pictured here was built in 1998 by McCoy Development as new construction, but was designed to have the look and appeal of a restoration. (Courtesy of David C. Lott.)

The Lone Oak Cabin is a prime example of a historic restoration. The cabin is one of six cabins in a grouping on West Lake Drive that were restored by architectural designer Charley Wright and builder David McCoy. All six cabins are currently rental units available to Medicine Park visitors. (Courtesy of David C. Lott.)

The unique beauty of Bath Lake has been the central drawing card for Medicine Park since its inception. This photograph shows another prime example of restoration of an early-1920s home located on West Lake Drive. (Courtesy of David C. Lott.)

Medicine Creek's two footbridges—the Curtis Davis Bridge, which spans Bath Lake, and the smaller one that connects the eastern creek bank with the island—were both rebuilt in the late 1990s. Both bridges were engineered and constructed as steel spans, and should be in place for many generations to come. (Courtesy of David C. Lott.)

The town of Medicine Park is fortunate to have many creative residents. Pictured here is Larry "Doc" Morefield in one of many old-time Buffalo Elixir Medicine Shows street theater performances periodically staged around town. Here he coaxes members of the audience into a few well-deserved laughs. In his spare time, Larry is a blacksmith and director of the radiology department at Grady Memorial Hospital in Chickasha. He built the old-time Medicine Show Wagon. (Courtesy of David C. Lott.)

The original main entry sign into Medicine Park was built prior to the 1920s. It is located on what is now Rex Leath Drive, which runs between the fish hatchery ponds on the north, and Medicine Creek to the south. The sign and its cobblestone columns were completely restored in early 2009. (Courtesy of David C. Lott.)

The year-round activities in Medicine Park include music festivals, mini-concerts, Marauder shootouts, medicine shows, art show openings, competitive cooking challenges, and trout fishing tournaments. Sponsored by the Park Tavern, the annual Polar Bear Plunge into Medicine Creek is held the first Saturday in February. What began a number of years ago with four people taking a dip into the icy waters has grown to as many as 200 people. (Courtesy of David C. Lott.)

Bob Wills had dozens of musicians pass through his Texas Playboys band over four decades. Bob passed on in 1975, but a few of his band members from the 1960s and 1970s keep the western swing music alive. This 2001 photograph from a dance at Medicine Park Music Hall features Grammy-winning Tommy Allsup on guitar (center) and lead vocalist Leon Rausch (center). It was Allsup who flipped a coin with Ritchie Valens for a seat on the airplane that would crash less than an hour later, killing Buddy Holly, Richie Valens, and J. P. Richardson Jr. (the Big Bopper). (Courtesy of David C. Lott.)

Local architectural designer Charley Wright (left) is often called Medicine Park's "Parkitech" because of his work on numerous historic property restorations. In late 2009, the town honored him for his design of almost 1 mile of lighted and landscaped creek-side walkway along Medicine Creek by naming it the Charley Wright Trails. In addition, they commissioned and dedicated a likeness of Charley by sculptor Robert Dean (right), and mounted it on a granite rock pedestal near Bath Lake. (Courtesy of Patty Ferguson.)

Robert E. Dean was one of Medicine Park's finest artists. He passed away on February 16, 2010, at age 62. In recent years, he became noted for his "heroic"-sized metal sculptures of wildlife. Robert always had a work in progress, and yet another idea on the drawing board. In this photograph, Robert was working on his creation of a mounted lion for a local commission. There are some 16 sculptures created by Dean in private collections in Medicine Park. Most can be seen from sidewalks and streets in town. Dean's last creation was an AT&T Wireless commission located on the corner of North Sheridan Road and Cache Road in Lawton. It features his interpretation of America's "first wireless communication system" of an American Indian two times life size kneeling on a rock and making smoke signals with a blanket and small fire. (Courtesy of David C. Lott Collection.)

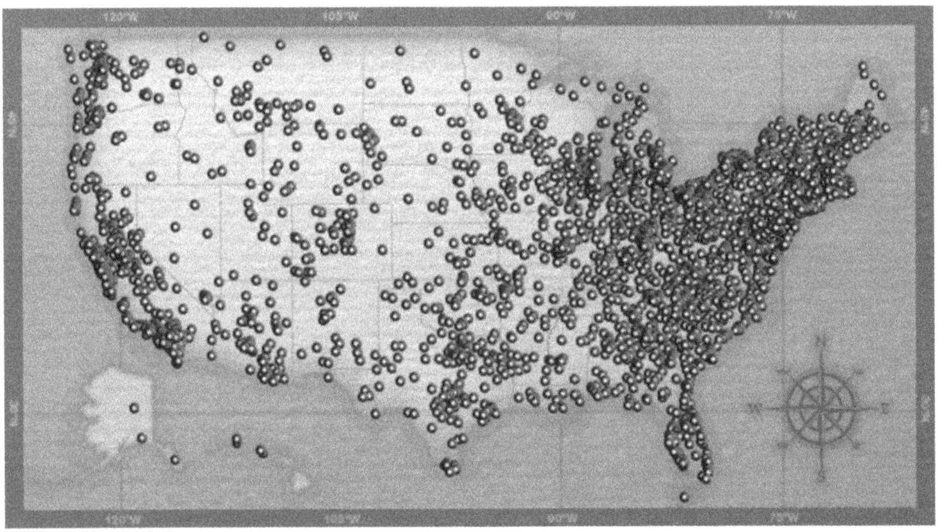

www.ingramcontent.com/pod-product-compliance
Lightning Source LLC
LaVergne TN
LVHW070819030926
847199LV00039B/507